General Giap

General
Giap

Politician and Strategist

Robert J. O'Neill

FREDERICK A. PRAEGER, *Publishers*
New York • Washington

BOOKS THAT MATTER
Published in the United States of America in 1969
by Frederick A. Praeger, Inc., Publishers
111 Fourth Avenue, New York, N.Y. 10003

© 1969 by Robert J. O'Neill. First published by
Cassell Australia Ltd., 1969.

Library of Congress Catalog Card Number: 69–12713

Printed in the United States of America

Contents

Plates

Viet Minh troops crossing Muong Thanh bridge for
the last attack on Dien Bien Phu
(*People's War, People's Army*)

The fall of Dien Bien Phu—10,000 French prisoners
(*Vietnam Peoples Army*)

Viet Minh soldiers hoist their flag atop de Castries'
bunker
(*Vietnam Peoples Army*)

A general view of Dien Bien Phu after the French
surrender

French liaison officers escort the first Viet Minh
troops entering the French lines, August 1954
(*Vietnam Peoples Army*)

Victory parade of Viet Minh artillery units in Hanoi
(*Vietnam Peoples Army*)

Acknowledgments are due to the following for permission to
reproduce photographs appearing in this book:

J. B. Lippincott Company, for plates 3, 4, 6, 11, 14 and 17,
from *Hell in a Very Small Place* by Bernard B. Fall, copyright
1966 by Bernard B. Fall; Camera Press, London, for plate 2;
Stackpole Books for plates 5 and 16, from *Street Without Joy*
by Bernard B. Fall; Faber and Faber Ltd, for plates 8, 9, 12
and 15, from *The Indo-China War, 1945-1954* by Edgar
O'Ballance and plate 13, from *The Battle of Dienbienphu* by
Jules Roy.

Maps and Diagrams

A number of these maps and diagrams have been repro-
duced by permission of the publishers, F. W. Cheshire,
from *Indo-China Tragedy 1945-1954* by Robert J. O'Neill.

Preface

This book has come into being through default of any comprehensive treatment of Giap in the two major roles for which he has achieved world notice. The availability of accurate information for the years 1912-57 is much greater than for the post 1957 period and so the latter part of Giap's life will await a historian's analysis for at least several years to come. The source material relating to Giap's early participation in the Communist movement, his activities during the Second World War and his leadership of the armed forces of the Viet Minh against the French has some gaps in it but there are sufficient established facts to enable the tracing in broad outline of his major activities, movements and rise to power. Some of the details of his life can be filled in, but until much more information becomes available it will not be possible to write a biography of Giap which will not require revision in some aspects from time to time.

The source material from which this book has been written consists largely of published information which will be familiar to most serious students of Vietnam in the twentieth century. As the *Note on Sources* (p. 205) shows, I have not disregarded any publication simply because it has come from Hanoi, or, for that matter, from any other place. The publications of the North Vietnamese Government contain, for the most part, so much bias, falsehood and exaggeration that they present acute problems to any historian who attempts to use them. However, this is not the case with all of Hanoi's publications, nor all of any one publication, as careful cross-checking with other sources will show. I have been assisted with background information by friends both in Vietnam and Australia who have had some first hand acquaintance with matters which I have treated and I am most grateful to those men whom I ought not to name in the present circumstances.

I hope that the reader's attention will be drawn to the constant interaction of political and military spheres of Giap's life, for it is this constant intermeshing of two threads, usually separated in Western societies, that has led to his continuing success and influence. Giap, of course, has shown great skill in coping with the requirements of such a many-sided life but had he been a member of a society which required him to confine his activities to a more narrow field, then it is possible that his career would have been relatively short-lived. Not only would he have lacked the military status to buoy his position when he was low in political influence or the political reputation to sustain his fortunes after suffering military reverses but he also would not have had the degree of political insight necessary to wage a war of insurgency so successfully over many years. He is a unique leader, and cannot be measured against conventional scales without severe risk of suffering either magnification or diminution in the process.

In discussing his military strategy I have tried to present in each case some outline of the situation which confronted Giap and to show the various courses of action which these situations offered him. To some old Vietnam hands these considerations may seem rather academic, but they have been included so that it is possible to assess Giap not only *ex post facto* by what his plans actually achieved, but also by the quality of the decisions which he took as the first step in achieving a military result. In some military operations there is a surprising disparity between these two appraisals. An interesting case in point is the strategy of guerrilla warfare. Giap has conducted this type of war very successfully, but it is necessary to know whether the Viet Minh adopted this method because of Giap's brilliant inspiration or whether they were forced to accept this method of operating because there was no other feasible possibility, before he can be assessed as a strategist as distinct from a tactician. Vietnam since 1945 has contained so many uncertainties and surprises for experts of all kinds that it has become accepted practice in many quarters to make no attempt to formulate solutions to the problems offered; mere criticism of failures or, to a much lesser extent, applause of successes, has been sufficient to produce reputations for strategic analysts both within and outside of government service. Remarks such as: 'Of course it was obvious that . . .' and 'I knew all along that . . .' have become so debased in value through over-use that one automatically unscrambles them from the value judgement which they imply and concentrates solely on the fact which follows them. Otherwise there seems to be no escape from the fallacy of interpreting every fact about war in Vietnam as a value judgement. In this treatment, I have tried to provide a comparison of facts from which value judgements can be made. Where I have not provided an array of facts, the reader might prosper by resisting the temptation to dispense the labels 'bad' and 'good'.

My thanks are due to many people for assistance with the production of this book: those who read the manuscript and offered comments, the cartographers, publishers and my wife Sally. A special mention is deserved by the final year history classes at Duntroon, Canberra, in 1967 and 1968 for their part in the discussions out of which many of the ideas in this book have grown.

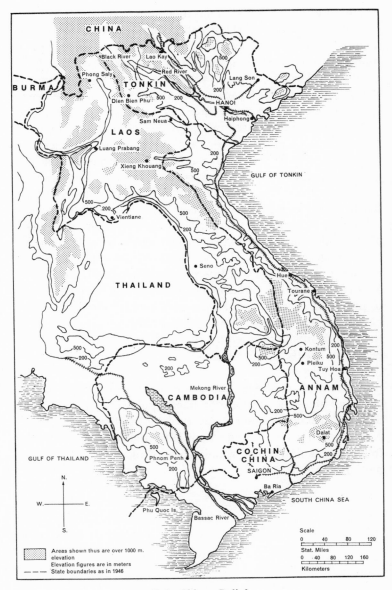

CHINA

Black River Lao Kay

Phong Saly Red River

500

BURMA Lang Son

TONKIN 200

Dien Bien Phu 500 200

HANOI

Sam Neua Haiphong

LAOS

Luang Prabang

200

Xieng Khouang 500

GULF OF TONKIN

500

200 Vientiane 500

200

Seno

Hue

THAILAND Tourane

Kontum 200

500 500

Pleiku Tuy Hoa

200

ANNAM

Mekong River CAMBODIA

200

500

Dalat

500

COCHIN 500

GULF OF THAILAND 500 CHINA 200

Phnom Penh SAIGON

200

N.

Ba Ria

W. E.

SOUTH CHINA SEA

S.

Phu Quoc Is.

Bassac River

Scale

0 40 80 120

Areas shown thus are over 1000 m. Stat. Miles
elevation
Elevation figures are in meters 0 40 80 120 160
State boundaries as in 1946 Kilometers

Indo China—Relief

1 The Making of a Propagandist

From his earliest years, Vo Nguyen Giap has lived in the midst of turbulent events concerned with the independence of his own country. Despite his subsequent association with the politics of Tonkin and North Vietnam, he was born in Central Annam in the village of An Xa in Quang Binh Province just to the north of the seventeenth parallel. Born in 1912, he lived in the general area between Hue and Dong Hoi until 1930, when he was imprisoned for the only time in his life by the French. In view of his familiarity with this region—currently of such strategic importance—it seems small wonder that he was reported to be directing North Vietnamese operations around the Demilitarized Zone in person in 1967 and 1968.

Giap's father was a scholar of distinction. He was accorded much respect by the people amongst whom he lived and taught, but he remained a poor man for the whole of his life. He could remember the days when the major cities of Northern Annam and Tonkin had been free of French rule and he had taken part in the great organized uprising against the French in the years between 1885 and 1888 which had been led by the Emperor Ham Nghi. The Emperor, however, was no more than a figurehead in the early years of this strife, for he was only thirteen years of age when the fighting commenced in 1885. The real leader of the revolt was a mandarin of the

Council of Regents, Ton That Thuyet, assisted by the great scholar and nationalist Phan Dinh Phung. These two received a great deal of assistance from the scholars of Annam who were able to give a local uprising the significance required to convert it into a national movement. These leaders quickly made their mark on the French and a French officer wrote of Le Truc, the rebel leader in the provinces of Quang Binh and Ha Tinh, 'This convinced patriot of simple and patriarchal

North Vietnam—Provinces

habits and of integrity in his high position was from every point a man to be respected.'[1]

One of the factors which contributed to the eventual capture of Ham Nghi through the treachery of a village chief, Trung Quang Ngoc, was the assistance which the small Catholic population of Central Annam gave to the French. It was this group which prevented the French from being completely isolated from the local people. They betrayed the hiding places of the rebels, provided a flow of information to the French soldiers and a ready source of coolie labour. To be fair to these Catholics, it must be noted that not only had they suffered severely from persecutions ordered by Emperor Minh Mang after 1820, but also the rebels had begun to terrorize them as soon as the fighting had broken out. Nonetheless, young Giap grew up in an atmosphere which regarded the Vietnamese Catholics as traitors with whom no compromise could be tolerated. He had also learned from the example of his father that a vital part of a national political movement was an intellectual content which could inspire the fervour of the peasants, channelling their grievances into forceful action against an oppressive government.

After the death of Phan Dinh Phung in 1895, the nationalist movement lapsed for five years until another dynamic leader, the young Phan Boi Chau, began to promote opposition to the French. In 1905, he was forced to flee to Japan, a popular refuge for Vietnamese nationalists, where he was joined a year later by Prince Cuong De. The Prince, a descendant of Emperor Gia Long who ruled Annam in the early nineteenth century, was Chau's choice as the future head of state of an independent Vietnam. They and their followers were encouraged and spurred on to greater action by the Japanese victory over the Russians in 1905.

One of the aims of these nationalists was to bring about a modern state through the replacement of traditional Confucianist upbringing by Western, scientific education. This issue was fought out during the years immediately preceding the

[1]Charles Gosselin, *L'empire d'Annam* (Perrin, Paris, 1904), p 271

4	GENERAL GIAP

birth of Giap. Most Vietnamese had resisted the pressures to break links with the past and had refused to send their children to the modern schools for the first generation of the French rule, but by 1907, demand for modern education had begun to grow. In the face of French refusal to build new schools the Vietnamese organized their own. The French suppressed these schools and imprisoned their initiators, sending for the first time hundreds of prisoners to the infamous island of Poulo Condore. However, these prisoners were not common vagabonds, but were many of the foremost intellectuals of their nation. Mass demonstrations, often accompanied by bloodshed, took place in Central Annam and the French yielded. The *Dong Kinh Nghia Thuc* or Private Schools Movement had been successful and more Franco-Vietnamese schools were opened. Vietnamese children were admitted to the *Lycée* at Hanoi and in 1918 the University of Hanoi, closed ten years earlier by the oppressive French Governor General Klobukowski, was reopened.

The year of Giap's birth, 1912, marked the commencement of a new era in Franco-Vietnamese relations. The last of the revolts led or assisted by the Nguyen Emperors had been crushed and no comparable armed insurrection on a large scale took place until the end of World War II. Despite the writings of some nationalist Vietnamese historians, the period 1912-44 was dominated by the spirit of collaboration with the colonial masters, either as a way to achieve independence or simply as a means of easing the difficulties of life. In 1914 and again in 1939, many Vietnamese joined the French Army to fight in the European and Mediterranean theatres of war. While a small number of revolts did occur during this period, and a few outstanding revolutionaries grew to maturity, these were exceptional events, standing out as isolated peaks above a misty valley of collaboration and indifference.

One of those who had organized the establishment of private schools during the early years of this century was Ngo Dinh Kha, father of Ngo Dinh Diem, Ngo Dinh Nhu and Ngo Dinh Thuc. By a strange irony, it was Ngo Dinh Kha who had helped to give Vo Nguyen Giap several years of his education. In 1924, Giap entered the *Lycée National* at Hue, following in the footsteps of both Ho Chi Minh, who attended school as Nguyen Tat Thanh, and Ngo Dinh Diem.

Internal politics in Vietnam had recovered from the doldrums of the World War I years and a number of new parties and movements dedicated to Vietnamese national independence grew up in the mid-twenties. The first of these was the legally formed Constitutionalist Party which grew up in the colony of Cochin China in 1917 assisted by the French as a type of safety valve. Aimed at moderate reforms, the Constitutionalist Party soon encountered strong French opposition. The Party was not prepared to sanction the mass use of violence for its ends, partly because its leaders felt vulnerable to these methods as much as the French, and the movement lost support. Those who were not content with the policy of moderate demands split away to form groups who were prepared to take a harder line, while those who remained in the Constitutionalist Party became little more than collaborators with the French. In 1924 an illegal party, the *Tan Viet Cach Menh Dang* or Revolutionary Association of Vietnam, known usually as the *Tan Viet*, was established in Annam. The *Tan Viet* quickly spread its influence into Tonkin, winning the support of young commercial employees and teachers. The *Tan Viet* was against the monarchy and endeavoured to promote the widening of education, but it failed to develop a clearly defined policy for the achievement of independence. Its attitude towards the burning question of revolution was much too moderate for the growing numbers of those who had been completely alienated from the French. Many of this latter group began in 1925 to join the newly-formed Revolutionary League of the Youth of Vietnam, the *Thanh Nien*, which had been organized by a Vietnamese attached to Michael Borodin's Soviet mission to China, Ly Thuy, better known as Ho Chi Minh.

One of Ho's first moves was to organize the betrayal to the French of Phan Boi Chau, one of the most important of the

Vietnamese nationalist leaders of the pre World War I era. Phan Boi Chau had fled to Canton to escape the French and had come to know Ho Chi Minh whom he refused to regard as a rival. Trusting naively in Ho's loyalty, Phan Boi Chau allowed himself to come within reach of French agents in Shanghai in June 1925 who had been tipped off by Ho in return for the huge sum of 100,000 piasters. Phan Boi Chau was transported back to Indo China, placed on trial by the French in Hanoi in November and sentenced to hard labour for life. He was pardoned a few weeks later by the newly arrived French Governor General, Varenne, and he spent the remaining fourteen years of his life confined to his house in Hue, isolated from contact with the outside world.

Vietnamese popular feeling, already severely agitated by the arrest and trial of Phan Boi Chau, was provoked into widespread demonstration of discontent by the death in March 1926 of Phan Chau Trinh, a scholar who had played a leading part in the private schools movement. Phan Chau Trinh had been saved by the League of Human Rights from a French prison in 1911 and had continued to agitate for a Vietnamese state free of French control in internal affairs and organized on republican lines. However he eschewed the use of violence and believed that the only road to independence lay through co-operation with the French. Although he failed to achieve much progress towards his goal, his death was widely mourned by the Vietnamese people who showed their grief in a number of ways including a harshly repressed strike by students throughout the country.

One of the principal organizers of the 'student movement' and of the great demonstration which followed the funeral of Phan Chau Trinh in Saigon was the *Tan Viet*, which was able to increase its strength appreciably through the growth of popular opposition to the French rule. Despite Phan Boi Chau's isolation in Hue, he was permitted visits from a number of apparently harmless schoolboys, including the fourteen year old Vo Nguyen Giap. The student strikes of 1925 and 1926 had awakened Giap's political consciousness and his keenness for action. His thoughts received inspiration from Phan Boi Chau who provided his young listeners with the penetrating commentaries on world events for which they hungered. During these years Giap also read the writings of the nationalist revolutionary in exile, Nguyen Ai Quoc or 'Nguyen the Patriot', another of the aliases of Ho Chi Minh. Giap's first acquaintance with Ho's thinking came through the pamphlet *Colonialism on Trial* which was circulated clandestinely in a cover printed in Arabic script. Giap records that to read for the first time a book denouncing colonialism inspired him with 'so much hatred and thrilled us.'[2]

After taking part in the 'quit school movement' organized by the students in Hanoi, Giap was expelled from the *Lycée National* and had to return to his native village, An Xa. Many students fled from Vietnam to China where they congregated in Canton, the centre for Vietnamese nationalists in exile. Amongst these emigrés was Pham Van Dong, a youth who was in his final year at school in Hanoi, and who was later to become Prime Minister of North Vietnam. Giap was very anxious to escape to Canton but the practical difficulties in the way of a fifteen year old boy defeated his intentions and he had to remain in Annam, relieving his frustrations by joining with others in secret nationalist agitation. One day he was visited by a close friend from Hue, Nguyen Chi Dieu, who enrolled Giap in the *Tan Viet*. By 1927, this organization had begun to split into two wings, one of which was Communist-oriented. It was this latter wing which Giap joined and he was given several pamphlets on Communism, including one printed in Brussels by the World League of Oppressed Peoples and another, a speech by Nguyen Ai Quoc. Giap, according to his own account, took these papers out into the fields, climbed a tree and studied them, finding great intellectual satisfaction in the idea of a total overthrow of the current order and in the principle of a peaceful international community linked by the bonds of Communism. Shortly afterwards, he was recalled to

[2]Vo Nguyen Giap, 'Ho Chi Minh, Father of the Viet Nam Revolutionary Army' in *Days With Ho Chi Minh* (Foreign Languages Publishing House, Hanoi, 1962), p. 184

Hue by the *Tan Viet* to carry out underground activities for the party.

While Giap had been making his connection with the *Tan Viet*, the *Thanh Nien*, or Revolutionary Youth League, established by Ho Chi Minh in 1925, had been progressing steadily. The flow of intelligent young men from Tonkin to Canton as a result of French repression of student activities had provided Ho with many lieutenants of the highest calibre. The best of these he kept in Canton to form the central committee of the *Thanh Nien* and to produce the party newspaper of the same name while the remainder were sent back to Vietnam to organize secret cells and to spread the party propaganda. Political circumstances in Vietnam favoured the growth of the *Thanh Nien* and it gathered together many of those who had become discontented with the more moderate policies of the Constitutionalist Party in Cochin China, the *Tan Viet* in Annam and the nationalists in Tonkin who were at that stage not organised into a cohesive body of opinion. Proximity to the sanctuary of China made Tonkin the easiest area for the Communists to operate and the *Thanh Nien* swiftly became a major contender for dominance of Tonkinese politics.

The *Thanh Nien* did not have things all its own way however, for in 1927 a new nationalist party, the *Viet Nam Quoc Dan Dang* or National Party of Vietnam, came to prominence in Hanoi. The VNQDD was based on lower middle class groups who were in many ways closer to the workers than the Communist leaders who were largely disaffected student sons of established families. Friction between the *Thanh Nien* and the VNQDD developed after the arrest of Phan Boi Chau, for the nationalists held Ho responsible for the episode. The Communists also suffered from a lack of funds which they attempted to make good by robbing any wealthy Vietnamese who happened to be convenient. This brigandry produced a reaction on the part of popular opinion which the colonial administration used as a licence to treat all Communists discovered as gangsters. The rift between Chiang Kai-shek and the Chinese Communists led to the cessation of Borodin's activities in Canton and Ho had to accompany him back to the Soviet Union where he remained until 1929. This left the Communist movement in Vietnam without strong leadership and the *Thanh Nien* split into two groups. A hard line group formed the Indo China Communist Party in 1927 and the remainder, frightened into a more provocative policy, organized itself into the Annamese Communist Party. Shortly afterwards, the elements in the *Tan Viet* who were inclined to follow a Communist line split away to form the Indo China Communist Union. All three of these Communist groups then proceeded to fight each other and the French police made good use of the opportunity to make extensive arrests of the members who were revealed by this strife.

After a short period in Berlin, Ho was sent back to South East Asia, where he was stationed in Bangkok to work under a French Communist, Hilaire Noulens. Appalled by events in Vietnam, Ho pleaded with the Comintern for authority to attempt to reunite the Communist movement there. After a year of waiting, he was allowed to proceed and at a conference which he called in Hong Kong in 1930 he succeeded in bringing the three groups together to form the Vietnamese Communist Party, which was expanded in the following year to become the Indo China Communist Party with responsibility for Vietnam, Laos and Cambodia.

French discovery of the clandestine activities of the VNQDD led the party leader, Nguyen Thai Hoc, to order preparations for a national uprising. When some of the bombs which were being made for the uprising were accidentally exploded the French realized at once what was going on and began arresting the leaders of VNQDD. Nguyen Thai Hoc felt that he dare not allow preparations to mature further for fear of French counter moves and he gave the order for the uprising to commence on 10 February 1930. Shortly afterwards he changed the day to 15 February but the party branch at Yen Bay, an important garrison town in Tonkin, did not receive the message and the rebellion began piece-meal. The French crushed it quickly, capturing and executing many of the VNQDD leaders, while the survivors escaped to China where they remained in a poor state of organization until 1945.

The Communists, who had been joined at this stage by Giap from the Communist wing of the *Tan Viet*, felt driven to continue the revolt and exploited the disastrous depression which had been enforced on Vietnamese agriculture by the world economic collapse. On May Day 1930 huge protest demonstrations were held which developed into riots. The French authorities responded by firing with machine guns on mobs in the main centres of population. Forced out of the cities, the Communists attempted to salvage the revolution by establishing Communist communities in those parts of the country which were still under their control, namely Nghe An and Ha Tinh provinces in Northern Annam, a movement which has become known as the Nghe An Soviets. French troops were brought in and the Soviets were crushed after a few months of bitter fighting. The Communist movement went underground, Ho was arrested in Hong Kong and Giap was sent to prison for three years.

A few months later Giap was released for good behaviour and he appeared to have turned over a new leaf. Perhaps the frustrations of prison life had encouraged him to take stock of himself with regard to his education and station in life. Whatever the cause, he devoted himself to his studies during the following eight years with a diligence which has produced a record establishing his claim to be regarded as an intellectual of high standing. After passing the difficult examinations of the French *Baccalaureat* in Hue he moved to Hanoi, then the outstanding centre of learning in Vietnam. He attended the *Lycée Albert-Sarraut* for an additional year of pre-university study. At the University of Hanoi, Giap studied law and political economy, taking his *licence en droit* in 1937, and going on to post graduate studies in 1938. His political activities began to become more demanding about this time for he had become involved in writing articles for several newspapers and periodicals which disseminated Communist thought in both

Vietnamese and French. A photograph taken in 1937 shows him working on the staff of the two Vietnamese language newspapers *Tin Tuc* or 'The News' and *Thoi The* or 'The Current Situation'. Because French language newspapers were subject to fewer controls than the Vietnamese language publications Giap also wrote for *Le Travail* and *Notre Voix*. *Le Travail* had been established by a group of intellectuals from several parties. For some time the paper succeeded in unifying all nationalists in Tonkin, but the growth of branches of the French Communist Party as a result of the greater freedom accorded to left wing parties by the Popular Front Government in France led to a resurgence of Communist activities and to a take-over by the Communists of *Le Travail*. While Giap was working for *Notre Voix* the editorial board often received articles from abroad signed P. C. Lin. These articles were given special priority for it was known that they were by Ho Chi Minh.

During these years of intense writing, Giap's studies began to suffer and he failed to take his Certificate of Administrative Law in 1938 nor did he, as some writers have claimed, take a doctorate in political economy.[3] At some point during these years he married the daughter of a professor at the University of Hanoi. Unable to continue full time studies beyond 1938 because of shortage of money, he became a teacher of history at the Thang Long private school in Hanoi.

Two outstanding young men whom he came to know through journalism in Hanoi were Pham Van Dong and Dang Xuan Khu, the latter better known by his alias, Truong Chinh or 'Long March'. Pham Van Dong had returned to Vietnam in 1926, only to be arrested shortly after his arrival and sentenced to six years imprisonment on Poulo Condore. After his release he went to Hanoi and gradually undertook further activities for the Communist Party, in particular journalism. Pham Van Dong met Giap through this work and a close friendship developed which was to be further strengthened by their

[3]Hoang Van Chi, *From Colonialism to Communism: A Case History of North Vietnam* (Frederick A. Praeger, New York, 1963), p. 69

adventures together in China during the Japanese occupation. Truong Chinh had also had a difficult life during the thirties. Jailed in 1930 after the unsuccessful uprisings he was not released until 1936. He was then unlucky enough to be caught by a French wave of repression which followed the Nazi-Soviet Pact of 1939 and was reincarcerated for a short time until he was able to make his escape to China where he was known to be early in 1941.

The shattering of the VNQDD in 1930 had left the Communists in a position of greater strength in Vietnam. However several Trotskyite parties in the South had reduced Communist strength in Cochin China. Several attempts were made in the mid-thirties to reconcile differences and to achieve greater co-operation between the Marxist parties but the Trotskyites in the South did not trust the Communists of the North. They mistakenly believed their basis of power in the South was adequate to ensure their survival as a strong party and they remained aloof from Ho's leadership.

It is interesting to look at the personal position which Giap had achieved by 1939. He had risen to share with only a few others the leadership of the strongest political organization in Vietnam. Apart from Ho Chi Minh, Pham Van Dong and Truong Chinh, who was at that time languishing in prison, there was no other leader who could rival Giap's position within the party. To have risen so far by the age of twenty-seven attested to Giap's ability. The man immediately above him in the party hierarchy, Pham Van Dong, was six years older than Giap and had had the advantage of personal contact with Ho in the mid-twenties to enhance his status. It was obvious that Giap, having risen to this level before he reached the height of his powers, was going to make a substantial contribution to the political history of his country during the next twenty or thirty years—provided that he survived the constantly threatening French legal system and any other calamities which befell Vietnam. For this reason the Communist Party had included Giap on its very short list of members who were to leave Vietnam should severe danger threaten their safety.

Lest it should be imagined that the success of the Communists in winning support throughout Vietnam was essentially due to the absence of rivals, it is important to examine the conduct of the internal political battle in Vietnam in the nineteen-thirties. After the abortive uprisings of 1930, most of the major parties suffered the loss of their leaders and the destruction of their local organizations in the densely populated areas. However, the Communists maintained a constant stream of young men through the training establishments available in the Soviet Union and China and so they were able to replace their leaders more easily than the other parties who did not have the advantage of outside assistance. These leaders had been taught to appreciate that the strength of a revolutionary movement was in the support of the peasants and workers. The fruits of the experience of the Soviet leaders were placed at the disposal of Ho's assistants, several of whom had been undergoing training in Moscow every year since 1925.

How did the Communists come to win so many young intellectuals from influential families? Why was Giap not throwing his support behind one of the less revolutionary groups who would preserve his social position through attempting the much more modest aims of a greater degree of independence for Vietnam, yet within the structure of French capitalism? The goals of the moderate nationalists offered many attractions to those of middle and upper class backgrounds because the availability of French capital would lead to increased opportunity for the educated and an almost guaranteed improvement in income. The stated aim of the Communists—total social and economic revolution—seemed to endanger much that the middle and upper classes already enjoyed.

The answer to this problem can be seen in the speeches of the non-Communist nationalist leaders of the early thirties. Even moderates such as Diem had come to denounce capitalism as an institution because they thought that it could never be made to work for the benefit of anyone but the French. The more frustrated the Vietnamese intellectuals became, the more they tended to be dragged by Francophobia to the extreme opposite of capitalism. Once this move had become established it became apparent to many young Vietnamese that capitalism offered no refuge for whatever inherited advantages they happened to enjoy and so in order to achieve what they could for themselves it seemed sensible to win some status within the organization which was attracting some of the most talented of the nation.

In Giap's case the Communist Party appeared to have been particularly enlightened in not attempting to tear him away from his studies and mental development before he had reached his limit. Certainly the times were such that this could be permitted. Had Giap been a few years older or younger then his academic development could have been cut short by the troubles of the early thirties or by the Japanese occupation and the French repression of Communists during the war years. During the years of his tertiary education, Giap was able to support himself to a moderate extent through his writings for Communist papers. Undoubtedly these arrangements also worked out to the advantage of the Communist Party but it is to the Party's credit that it waited patiently, avoiding the risk of damaging the quality of the final product.

The success of the Indo China Communist Party during the thirties depended on more than the quality of its leadership. While the other nationalist parties concentrated their appeal on the 'leading elements' of society, the intelligentsia, the officials, the business men and the skilled craftsmen, the Communists directed themselves at the lowest levels of the social order. The moderates felt that the peasants had nothing to contribute to the independence movement and therefore they were largely irrelevant. Some saw themselves as heroes, fighting on behalf of the mute masses, others were cynical enough to feel that if they achieved independence without the support of the peasants they would owe the lower orders of society nothing.

The Communists, on the other hand, knew from their readings of Marx, Engels and Lenin that not only was the Vietnamese economy being controlled by foreign capital, but that it was in the stages of early capitalism in which the peasants had not begun to receive any of the benefits of an advanced capitalist society. It is interesting to speculate on the outcome of the passage of a Western European nation through the industrial revolution in the presence of organized international Communism. The Communists felt that eventually they would have to challenge the French by physical force for control of Vietnam and so they spoke out for the grievances of the masses, held out solutions for their plight and won the support, or at least the goodwill, of urban and rural poor throughout Vietnam, although with particular concentration on Central and Northern Annam and the Red River delta.

It is important to remember these factors when considering the state of mind of the Communist leaders in Vietnam in the late thirties. By 1939 they knew that they were in a position of strength and they could feel the thrilling presence of a destiny which seemed to be leading them inevitably towards the realization of political power. The only obstacle in their path seemed to be the French Army, but it was apparent to skilful observers of the international scene that two other challenges to French military power were arising: Nazi expansionism in Europe and Japanese chauvinism in East Asia. It was impossible to foretell the outcomes of these confrontations but to Ho and his colleagues, 1939 must have appeared pregnant with favourable opportunities which could lead with perceptive handling to a military vacuum in Vietnam—the only remaining prerequisite for the successful seizure of power by the Communists.

The French repressive measures which followed the Nazi-Soviet pact produced a wave of anxiety amongst the higher Communist ranks for they had become accustomed to the greater freedom which the years of the French Popular Front government had produced and as a result, they had become a little less secretive in their methods of operation. Giap and

Pham Van Dong knew that they were under daily supervision by the *Sûreté* and Ho became increasingly worried about the security of his leading supporters. Fortunately for them the French had other preoccupations in Indo China as the possibilities of war with Japan began to threaten.

In November 1939, the Japanese launched a strong offensive in Southern China and captured the city of Nanning, 147 miles from the Tonkinese border by road or only a few hours of motoring away from the key French fort of Lang Son which protected the *Porte de Chine*. This left China with only the Burma Road and the Hanoi-Kunming railway for outlets to the sea and supply routes for vital foreign assistance to flow to Chiang Kai-shek. Obviously the next Japanese thrust would be aimed at Indo China in order to cut the railway. The Japanese advance was then checked by internal political changes which followed the fall of the Hiranuma Government as a result of the loss of face suffered by Japan over the Nazi-Soviet pact. The more moderate governments of General Abe and Admiral Yonai, who succeeded Abe in January 1940, led to a policy designed to preserve neutral relations with Europe while the war in China was continuing.

However, the German successes in Norway in April 1940 indicated that France's hour of trial was approaching, making it harder for the Japanese to resist the temptations of occupying Indo China in order both to cut the railway to China and to enjoy the economic spoils of the country. Ho knew that, after the Anti Comintern pact, the Japanese-Russian border conflicts and the resistance offered by the Chinese Communists to the Japanese, it would be foolhardy to expect tolerance of the Indo China Communist Party by a Japanese army of occupation and so he summoned his lieutenants in Hanoi to join him in Yunnan.

Giap and Pham Van Dong were to leave Hanoi together on 4 May 1940. Pham Van Dong was ill at that time and Giap found it difficult to be absent from his school-teaching duties for any period of time without the knowledge of the *Sûreté*. By teaching on Friday, 3 May, he was able to get the weekend free and so by leaving on Saturday he and Pham Van Dong would have two days in which to flee as far as possible without discovery. Giap farewelled his wife and sister, neither of whom he was to see again. His wife was jailed by the French and died in 1943, of illness, according to the French, and of mal-treatment, according to Giap. His sister was guillotined for her political activities. From that time onwards Giap was never without the strongest personal motives for opposing colonial rule. The French who negotiated with Giap in 1945 and 1946 dubbed him 'the ice-covered volcano'. Certainly they had only their compatriots to blame for much of his hatred.

On the Friday evening, Giap was taken by devious routes in a rickshaw pulled by a trusted friend through the suburbs of Hanoi to a safe location for the night. On the following day he went with Pham Van Dong to the End-of-the-Bridge station in time to catch the train for Lao Kay, the border station en route to Kunming and Ho Chi Minh.

2 Military Beginnings

Giap and Dong were setting out to travel the length of a railway line which had been one of the greatest white elephants of the colonial era. Paul Doumer, Governor General of French Indo China from 1897 to 1902, had fought with determination for two great rail links which would, he hoped, transform the economy of Indo China by making it the natural outlet for the South China trade. One line joined Hanoi and Saigon, competing inefficiently with the adequate sea route between the two cities. The other linked Haiphong with Kunming, capital of Yunnan, via the natural communications route of the Red River valley. The lines were planned without thought to whether the country was in a sufficient state of economic development for the railways to be even of some small use, let alone run at a profit. Their construction was marred by poor planning, swindles, public scandals and high fatalities. Out of the 80,000 Chinese and Vietnamese labourers who worked on the Red River line, 25,000 died during its construction.

By 1903 the line had reached the edge of the Red River delta. During the following three years it was forced up the fever ridden valley which cleaves with such remarkable straightness the mountains of Tonkin, which tower above the river to a height of up to ten thousand feet. The slender metre gauge was taken across the Nan-ch'i River just over the

Chinese border to Ho-K'ou by a ferry and up the Nan-ch'i valley, reaching Meng-Tzu, three hundred miles from Hanoi, in 1906. The remaining 130 miles to Kunming were completed in 1910 at a total cost of 165,000,000 francs, nearly twice the initial estimate.

The hazards of the journey in the wet season when the countless tributaries of the Red River swirled around and plucked at the flimsy piles of the railway bridges were increased by the possibility of Japanese air attack on the line and by frequent police checks of the passengers. Twice during the journey, Giap and Dong had to hide while the train was searched. At Lao Kay, the Tonkinese town on the border, they had to change to a Chinese train after crossing the Nan-ch'i River on a bamboo raft. The journey to Kunming was even more risky than the stage just covered because the train was searched even more frequently. Every time that Giap and Dong saw railway officials or police boarding the train they moved quickly into the carriages which had been searched first and so kept eluding the minions of Chiang Kai-shek. There were sufficient Vietnamese refugees in South China for Giap and Dong to remain relatively inconspicuous once they had reached friends in Kunming who told them to wait for further instructions from a certain Mr Vuong.

Ho Chi Minh, after his release from prison in Hong Kong in 1933, had been given refuge in Moscow for five years where he studied at the Lenin School, a high level institution for leaders from abroad, and conducted courses for Vietnamese students at the National and Colonial Research Questions Institute. Late in 1938 he returned to Yunnan via Mao Tse-tung's headquarters in Yenan and Hanyang, making contact with local agents near the Sino-Tonkinese border in early 1940. Ho kept on the move fairly constantly during this period, and very few of the senior party officials in China had any idea that they were meeting with the man they had come to revere as Nguyen Ai Quoc.

Ho was assisted by the chaotic state of affairs which existed in Southern China as a result of the Japanese offensive. Chiang

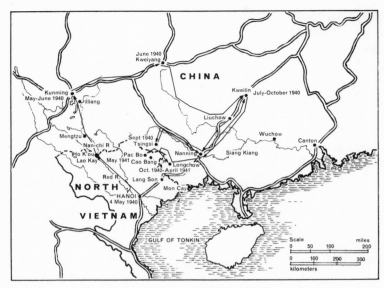

Giap's Travels in China, 1940-41

Kai-shek's officials were too distracted by the war to be able
to devote much attention to rounding up Vietnamese Communists, the Chinese Communists were present in the area in
sufficient strength to provide assistance to Ho, and the Japanese had so little control over the countryside behind their own
lines that the area was virtually a no-man's land, dominated by
several local war lords.

The Chinese Communists gave a great deal of assistance to
the newly arrived Vietnamese refugees. Giap and Dong were
provided with accommodation, books, writing materials and
a communications system by their Chinese comrades. Giap
still found life extremely hard, having to do his own shopping
and cooking. He claims that his culinary efforts were so dismal
that after his first attempts, his colleagues decreed that he
should discharge his share of the domestic duties as a permanent dish washer.

After some few weeks of waiting in Kunming, Giap and
Dong were told that Vuong was ready to see them. Vuong was,

of course, the leader whom they had admired from a distance for so long—Nguyen Ai Quoc or Ho Chi Minh. On a midsummer's day in early June, they were taken to the Tsuy-Hu River, where Ho and Vu Anh were waiting in a boat. At the approach of Dong and Giap, Ho stepped out on to the bank. They knew at once from photographs whom they were meeting. Ho teased them, 'Dong is not really getting old', 'Giap is still beautiful like a girl'.[4]

Several days of widely ranging discussions with Ho followed, during which Ho must have been impressed with the potential of the two younger men, for in late June he sent them on their way to Yenan, primarily to attend a political course but also to gain some knowledge of military techniques. Shortly after Giap and Dong had set out for Yenan with a third, Cao Hong Lanh, Paris fell to the Germans. Ho felt that this would greatly change the situation in Vietnam and he sent Vu Anh after them to recall them to Kweilin, preparatory to returning to Vietnam. Vu Anh caught up with the other three at Kweiyang, a three day journey from Kunming, where they were being looked after by the Chinese Communist Eighth Route Army until transport to Yenan was available. They went to Kweilin and awaited further instructions from Ho Chi Minh.

In the meantime, the Japanese had decided to exploit France's weakness and had demanded right of passage for their troops through Tonkin to attack China. The French gave way, and allowed the Japanese to enter in late September. Just to teach the French a lesson, the Japanese stormed the fortress of Lang Son on 22 September 1940. Shortly afterwards, 35,000 Japanese troops entered Indo China, and although the French were permitted to continue their administration, it became increasingly obvious that the new rulers of Indo China were the Japanese. The two Communist uprisings in Tonkin and in Cochin China which broke out in late 1940 were put down by the French and the various groups of nationalists in

'Vu Anh, 'From Kunming to Pac Bo', in *Days With Ho Chi Minh, op. cit.,* p. 167

Vietnam saw that the Japanese occupation had not solved the problem of how to achieve practical power.

From Kweiyang the small group travelled nearly two hundred and fifty miles east to Kweilin with the assistance of the Chinese Communists. The Nationalist commander in Kweilin, General Li Chi-shen, discussed with them the possibility of Nationalist troops entering Indo China, ostensibly for the expulsion of the Japanese. When Ho Chi Minh arrived in Kweilin and learned of the discussions, he reminded them that only the Soviet and Red Chinese Armies were to be considered their allies, and that the armies of Chiang Kai-shek were dangerous. The Vietnamese became increasingly apprehensive as their stay in Kweilin lengthened. Chiang had launched an offensive against the local Red Chinese Fourth Army and the Communist refugees from Vietnam felt that they might be arrested at any moment.

While the Communist leaders were making their plans in Kweilin, another few Vietnamese were organizing a military force with Chinese Nationalist co-operation near the Tonkinese border. The leaders of the force were two officers of Chiang Kai-shek's Army, Truong Boi Cong and Ho Ngoc Lam. Their chief supporter was General Chang Fa-k'uei, the Nationalist commander of the south-eastern border region of China. Ho felt that this group warranted a close look and Giap was sent to make contact with them at the town of Tsingsi, some twenty miles from the Tonkinese border. After some short time, a spy reported Giap's Communist activities in Tsingsi to the local Chinese Nationalist leaders, who at once changed their attitudes towards him.

Another top level conference of the Vietnamese Communists was held at Kweilin in October 1940 to discuss plans for the eventual return to Vietnam. Of particular relevance were the questions of how much co-operation should be attempted with Truong Boi Cong's group and to what extent it would be necessary to submerge Communism in a wider nationalist front in order to win sufficient popular support to govern the country. Apparently Truong Boi Cong or a representative was at this conference, for a merger of the two organizations was achieved under the title of Ho Ngoc Lam's earlier group, the League for the Independence of Vietnam, which had been founded in Nanking.

During the conference, news came through from Vietnam of the unsuccessful uprisings against the Japanese and the French. Many of the insurgents in Tonkin had been able to escape into China and they had met up with Truong Boi Cong. Giap returned to Tsingsi and made contact with the new refugees. It is at this stage that we can see the beginnings of Giap's military career, for these men became his first troops. He did not stop his writing and propaganda work, nor did he permit his military responsibilities to take him out of the main stream of politics, but from late 1940 onwards, he had begun to assume the burden of military command and had to devote his thinking to tactics, strategy, equipment, supplies, training and recruiting.

Giap gathered together forty cadre members of the Communist Party who had been with Truong Boi Cong and ran a course in minor tactics and guerrilla work for several weeks in the areas of Tsingsi, Longchow and Ca Ma, a small village just on the Chinese side of the border and north of the Tonkinese town of Cao Bang. Nowhere in his writings does Giap make mention of considering any alternative strategy to that of guerrilla warfare to achieve his aims. In the light of his knowledge of earlier Vietnamese tactics against the French—particularly those of Phan Dinh Phung and Hoang Hoa Tham—and of the methods of Mao Tse-tung, it is highly probable that he concentrated on guerrilla methods almost by instinct rather than by an unprejudiced rejection of the methods of conventional warfare.

Ho attended this course in a general supervisory capacity, and it is not unlikely that Giap received lessons in military techniques from the older man who had been trained for several years in Moscow and had twenty years of experience of defiance of superior forces. During the course, Ho sent Vu Anh back into Tonkin to look for a suitably inaccessible hiding place from which Ho could direct the first phase of taking control of the country. Vu Anh selected a cave well concealed amongst many others high on the slopes of a mountain a few miles south of the border in an area called Pac Bo. A short distance away was the French post at Soc Giang, and twenty miles to the south east lay the provincial capital of Cao Bang. Ca Ma was less than ten miles to the north by jungle trails which wound through the rugged border mountains.

After celebrating the Lunar New Year, *Tet*, in February 1941, Ho Chi Minh returned to his native land after an absence of thirty years. Giap and Dong remained behind in Tsingsi to continue their work of organizing groups of men who were to go back into Tonkin. It had been decided to hold a meeting, the eighth, of the Central Committee of the Indo China Communist Party at Pac Bo in May 1941 in order to shape the policies for the coming crucial years, and so the men in the caves and huts on either side of the border had a busy few months ahead.

During the first year of the Japanese occupation of Vietnam, several of the small political groups were forced to conceal their activities from the foreigners and their leaders eventually had to flee to China. These groups consisted mainly of moderate and conservative nationalists who were opposed to the Communists. In early 1941 they came together to form one of Vietnam's major political parties, the *Dai Viet Quoc Dan Dang* or Nationalist Party of Great Vietnam, usually referred to as the *Dai Viet*. A third Vietnamese political force in Southern China in 1941 was the remnant of the VNQDD under Vu Hong Khanh. The Chinese Nationalists had treated their Vietnamese *protégés* well and Vu Hong Khanh had received a great deal of military aid. However after the Communists had shown their efficiency in military organization and Ho had indicated a readiness to co-operate with Chiang Kai-shek in some matters, the Chinese Nationalists began to devote more assistance to the Communists and a bitter rivalry sprang up between the supporters of Ho Chi Minh and the Vietnamese Nationalists.

The Eighth Congress of the Indo China Communist Party began at Pac Bo in mid May 1941. The plenum, chaired by Ho, decided on 19 May to form a national front named the Vietnam Independence League or *Viet Nam Doc Lap Dong Minh Hoi*, better known as the *Viet Minh*. In view of the formation of Truong Boi Cong's organization of similar name, it seems that the true significance of the establishment of the Viet Minh was as a take-over of an organization in which the Communists had already been participating. The plenum also decided that the next task was to build two guerrilla bases further to the south at Bac Son and Vu Nhai so that the three provinces of Cao Bang, Lang Son and Bac Kan could be penetrated by the Viet Minh troops.

The Communist leaders spent most of late 1941 at Pac Bo, sometimes fleeing from French patrols which came up into the mountains from Soc Giang; they endured conditions of great physical hardship, not the least of which was a penetrating chill in the damp air. Notwithstanding, the Viet Minh were well enough organized to be able to care for their immediate material needs: food, shelter, medicines, training materials and facilities for producing a news sheet, *Viet Nam Doc Lap*, known usually as *Viet Lap*. During his stay in Tsingsi, Giap had published a longer, lithographed paper containing detailed and complicated articles which he had spent much effort in writing. After his arrival at Pac Bo, Giap asked Ho what he thought of his paper. Ho replied that he received it but no-one could be bothered to wade through Giap's lengthy articles. *Viet Lap* was published in large type and featured short articles of 100 words or less. Giap wrote the general news content and specialized articles on warfare, polemics attacking the French and Japanese and reports on women's activities.

Pac Bo became inadequate for controlling the steadily growing activities of the Viet Minh and after a few months the headquarters was moved to Lam Son, some thirty miles closer to the centre of Cao Bang province. The official function of the headquarters group was that of an advisory committee, appointed by the Central Committee of the Party, to assist the

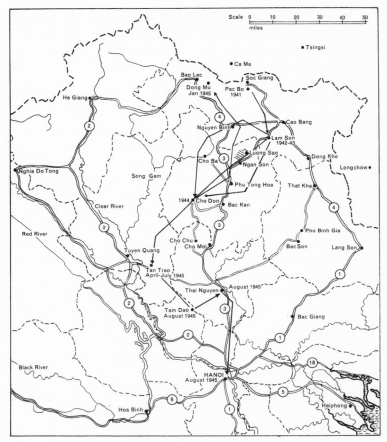

Giap's Progress, Pac Bo—Hanoi, 1941-45

Interprovincial Party Committee of Cao Bang, Lang Son and
Bac Kan provinces. The move to Lam Son posed greater
security problems for Giap because French patrols came
through this area more frequently. Evidently the military
organization of the Viet Minh was able to cope with the added
dangers for although many of Giap's men were captured, the
headquarters was able to keep functioning in the area until
sufficient control had been established over areas further south
to enable another move to an even more favourable area.

The strength of the Viet Minh forces had grown to three platoons, or some hundred soldiers, by late 1941. The French launched a sweep against the Bac Son platoon, causing the Viet Minh some serious losses as they fought their way out of the area. One of Ho's most valuable assistants, Phung Chi Kien, perished in a hillside ambush at Luong Sao, twenty miles south-west of Cao Bang.

Large numbers of Tonkinese began to join the Viet Minh after the move to Lam Son, and Giap found that he had to conduct recruit training courses for over fifty persons each month. Soon numbers became too great to concentrate all the trainees together so Giap had to organize mobile teams of instructors to go around the countryside, imparting instruction at a number of centres. Giap applied himself to learning several of the local mountain languages to help unify the diverse groups of tribesmen and town dwellers from whom his forces were slowly being formed.

Ho was very satisfied with progress in the Cao Bang area, and by early 1942 felt that the situation permitted him to return to China to renew his contacts with people who might provide assistance. Shortly after crossing the border, he was arrested by the Chinese Nationalists and taken before General Chang Fa-k'uei, who imprisoned him. The initial pretext for Ho's arrest was that he had no identification or other papers permitting him to travel through the zone controlled by the *Kuo Min Tang*. However, Chang Fa-k'uei certainly knew who Ho was and what his business was. Hence it seems likely that the Viet Minh were at that time out of favour with Chang Fa-k'uei and possibly with the Nationalist Government in Chungking. The Chinese had made plans for their own occupation of Tonkin, and they must have been aware of the progress Ho had been making in winning local support in the border areas of Vietnam. Ho had not troubled to preserve good relations with the Chinese Nationalists, and so the Chinese must have welcomed the chance to teach him a lesson and to exert some pressure on him to include politicians sympathetic to the aims of the *Kuo Min Tang* amongst his higher ranks.

The Viet Minh had previously made some offers of intelligence concerning Japanese activities in Tonkin to the *Kuo Min Tang,* in return for military assistance. The latter wanted this service but they did not wish to contribute to the strength of Communist trouble makers poaching on their own preserves and so had refused to give any aid. As time went by, the failure of the other Vietnamese nationalist groups to achieve any useful military role against the Japanese inclined the *Kuo Min Tang* to a compromise. If the Viet Minh would join with the other, non-Communist, groups in one united front and cease terrorizing their rival compatriots, the *Kuo Min Tang* would be prepared to render assistance to the Vietnamese and release Ho Chi Minh.

A conference of all Vietnamese groups represented in Southern China was called at Liuchow in October 1942. On 10 October the formation of the united front, the *Viet Nam Cach Minh Dong Minh Hoi,* or Vietnam Revolutionary League, known usually as the *Dong Minh Hoi,* was announced. The Viet Minh had to accept the leadership of an elderly nationalist, Nguyen Hai Than, a former associate of Phan Boi Chau who had lived in China for so many years that his speech had come to include many Chinese turns of phrase. During the following months it became obvious to the *Kuo Min Tang* that the *Dong Minh Hoi* was capable of doing little against the Japanese, for the Viet Minh had refused to give full co-operation.

Ho had not yet been released from prison. When he finally agreed to order the Viet Minh to co-operate with the *Kuo Min Tang* troops, he was freed in Liuchow in 1943. The relative military superiority of the Viet Minh, compared with the other Vietnamese groups, had played a vital part in Ho's release, so he had a great deal to thank Giap for on his return to Tonkin.

During Ho's period in prison, Pham Van Dong had taken over the political leadership of the Viet Minh and had been the leader of the Communist delegation to the Liuchow conference. Giap had been left to concentrate on his newspapers and his military training. By the end of 1943 he had several hundred young people in his 'shock operative groups', the National Salvation Army. His armed propaganda teams and regular platoons had extended their control over most of the provinces of Cao Bang, Lang Son and Bac Kan by working gradually along two parallel axes to the south, which finally linked up at the hamlet of Nghia Ta, near Cho Don. Nghia Ta was then called 'Victory Village' and a celebration was held. At the *Tet* festivities at Giap's headquarters, over twenty groups of 'Southward Marchers' were represented.

French activities against the Viet Minh were stepped up in 1944 and a series of determined operations was launched which lasted for several months. The French arrested many Viet Minh cadres and guerrillas and began to move village populations into areas which could be controlled more easily. Giap responded by strengthening not his military formations but his propaganda teams in order to preserve the popular will to resist the French until their offensive petered out. Important local leaders of the Viet Minh were smuggled out of the areas under French control and were sheltered in the mountain bases.

Once the propaganda teams had achieved their effect it was easy for Giap to form several new platoons and sections in the various districts which were being disputed. These groups continued to spread Giap's propaganda but they began to make the French feel their presence through setting ambushes for small patrols. They exerted a powerful influence on the local people by killing and torturing those who had offered the French any co-operation.

The success of Viet Minh actions in Tonkin made it possible for small bands of Giap's propagandists to arouse or reactivate Communist cells throughout the length of Vietnam. While the strength of the Communist Party was low after so many years of relative inactivity on a nation-wide basis, Giap at least had the beginnings of a command structure which would enable decisions reached in northern Tonkin to be put into effect in the Central Highlands of Annam and in the Mekong Delta. Provided that his cells could preserve their existence he could foresee the time when he could have an overstretched enemy reacting madly to his stings, wearing itself out through valiant attempts to quell disturbances first in one part of the country then in another and never getting the chance to employ superior fire power against a worthwhile concentration of troops.

The *Kuo Min Tang* made another attempt to cut back the power of the Viet Minh by forming a republican government for Vietnam at an all-party conference held at Liuchow in March 1944. The Viet Minh were given only one position in this government, but this arrangement worked to their advantage. After the conference, the only party delegation to return to Vietnam was that of the Viet Minh. The others remained in China to await the expected Allied offensive to expel the Japanese. The Viet Minh were thus able to claim before the Vietnamese people that they were the sole representatives of both the *Dong Minh Hoi* and the national government in exile which had the support of all nationalist parties. The Viet Minh were careful to maintain this attitude for several years and as a result they won the support and co-operation of many non-Communist nationalists.

Although Ho Chi Minh had been released from prison in 1943, the Chinese had insisted that he stay in Liuchow and it was not until late 1944 that he was able to return to Vietnam. The liberation of Paris and the installation of the de Gaulle regime in France provoked an outburst of optimism amongst the Viet Minh. They could see that this would sharpen the antagonism between the Japanese and the French and lead to the Japanese taking firm action against the French, thereby creating favourable circumstances for the growth of the Viet Minh. Once the Japanese had been expelled by the Allies, the Viet Minh would be able to step into the void and take control of Vietnam. Consequently, at a conference held in July 1944, Giap made preparations for nation-wide guerrilla warfare.

When Ho returned he rebuked Giap for his action and countermanded his orders, because none of the provinces out-

side the Cao Bang - Lang Son - Bac Kan area were ready for
involvement in fighting. Ho then ordered Giap to form the
first part of the National Liberation Army, the Vietnam
Liberation Unit. In order to stress the need for military
restraint at that time, Ho renamed this unit the Vietnam
Propaganda and Liberation Unit. Notwithstanding his concern to avoid large military encounters, he felt that it was
important from propaganda considerations to achieve a small
military victory over the French before the end of 1944.

Giap returned to his men and selected thirty-four to form
the first unit of the National Liberation Army. This, the first
Viet Minh main force unit, completed the three layer structure
which has been the basis of Communist organization in Vietnam ever since. Beneath the main force units came the District
Armed Groups and at the lowest level were the Village Self
Protective Groups which were only partly armed. These three
types of unit created a special command problem of co-ordination: for example, the villages could order their groups to
undertake some operation which might not suit the plans of the
district units. On Ho's advice, Giap unified the command
structure so that all initiatives came from the highest level.
This must have made life rather tedious for the village
guerrillas who were at the end of a very long and tenuous
chain of command.

Two days after the formation of the Propaganda and
Liberation Unit, the chosen thirty-four set about winning the
modest success which Ho wanted. They made two attacks on
small French outposts in the Viet Minh area, Khai Phat and
Na Ngan, on 24 December 1944. The attacks completely overcame the defenders and Giap's men captured badly needed
weapons, and even more badly needed ammunition. The birthday of the unit, 22 December, is now celebrated as the official
birthday of the People's Army of Vietnam.

After these attacks, Giap increased the size of his main force
to that of a company, and moved northward to attack the outpost of Dong Mu, near Bao Lac, on the border thirty miles
north-west of Cao Bang. As they went, the Viet Minh marched

openly through the mountain villages, showing the flag with great success. As soon as Giap felt that the French suspected the Viet Minh main force of the attack on Dong Mu, he withdrew a considerable distance to another prepared base in which he celebrated *Tet*, 1945.

The Japanese had been growing increasingly hostile towards the French during 1944, and the latter had been at no pains to conceal a reciprocal attitude. The clear turn of the tide caused the Japanese to take strong action against the French in order to establish a puppet Vietnamese regime which the former could control more easily, and which might lead after the war to a weakening of the European hold on the East Asian area of Japanese economic interest. On 9 March 1945 the Japanese attacked, killing or imprisoning the French troops and dismissing the civil administration. The Japanese had few garrisons outside the major towns and so the disappearance of the French created a vacuum of civil authority. Giap moved his main force further to the south, collecting recruits from village and district units he encountered on his way. By mid 1945, Giap had several thousands troops under his command and he stood on the threshold of generalship.

During the years 1940-5, Giap went through a transformation from a political writer and organizer to a military commander. From what we know of Giap in 1940, it is difficult to see why his career changed its pattern so abruptly and why it was he, rather than Pham Van Dong or Truong Chinh or someone else, who became Ho's general. However there are a number of factors which must be taken into account. Giap had always had some interest in military problems, he was a student of military history, and he seemed to have many of the traits of leadership and organizational ability needed by a commander. In the top level structure of the Indo China Communist Party only two men were clearly ahead of Giap in 1940 —Ho and Dong. These two had known each other well for a long time, and it seemed only natural that Dong became Ho's deputy for political affairs. The next most important position in the hierarchy was that of military commander, and had Giap not oriented himself for this position he might have ended up with considerably less power than he has held. Military work had to be accompanied by a great amount of propaganda activity, especially in the early stages. Giap was well suited by his background and talents to combine both types of work, and so Ho Chi Minh probably found the selection of Giap as his military commander a fairly straightforward matter.

Giap's thought must have matured greatly during these years of new activity. Giap has sometimes boasted that the only military academy which he attended was that of the bush. While this is true, it must be said that the bush is not a bad sort of academy in which to train a soldier. In particular given a few years, he can start from the smallest groups of troops and work upwards, with a live enemy who does not have to be taken too seriously, and under training conditions which permit a young cadet to accept some casualties amongst his own troops as he learns. The main deficiency of the bush as a military academy is that it has an inadequate library, and so one can learn little from the thoughts of others. Had Giap been able to study the great strategists while he developed his tactics, he might have avoided one or two of the pitfalls awaiting the feet of any eager soldier who does not understand the difference between a direct and an indirect approach.

We see Giap in mid 1945 as an officer with the background of a major, about to commence the tasks of a major general. At the same time his political training and responsibilities were far in excess of those normally associated with a major general, and thus his suitability for the sort of war he was about to fight was of a much higher order than that implied by the often repeated fact that Giap was a school teacher.

3 The Fortunes of Politics

Despite the hardships of the war years, Giap had experienced a steady consolidation and expansion of his power within the Communist movement. The coming of peace did much to ease his physical discomforts, but in the immediate post-war years Giap was to be tried by a series of political rises and falls which must have made him feel something of a pawn in the game of Vietnamese politics. The closeness of his link with Ho Chi Minh must have given him considerable reassurance, if any were needed, helping him to weather these rises and falls. The only permanent mark which this period seems to leave on Giap is a bitter hatred of those groups to whom Ho had felt obliged to sacrifice him in order to hold his governments together.

The disappearance of the French from the countryside after 9 March 1945 permitted the Viet Minh to move their headquarters further to the south, from Lam Son to Tan Trao, a small village between Tuyen Quang and Thai Nguyen, some sixty miles north-west of Hanoi. In May, Ho Chi Minh returned to Tonkin from a short visit to China, and Giap hastened north to meet him at Ha Kien. After enquiring into Giap's stewardship during his absence, he joined the headquarters at Tan Trao. Ho felt that the existing Viet Minh organization, which consisted of six provincial committees, ought to be tightened by the formation of a Liberated Area with oversight of the activities of these committees. A conference was summoned to consider this decision but, because of their operational commitments, the delegates from the provinces were unable to attend and Giap had to take on the function of permanent head of the Liberated Area Command.

Only in the final months of the war did the Viet Minh harass the Japanese in Indo China, and even then, the probable motives for these attacks were connected with the desire to be one of the victorious Allies after the Japanese had been defeated. The only major engagement recorded between the Japanese and the Viet Minh was in the Tam Dao mountains, a long spine of high ground which rises out of the north-west corner of the Red River delta to a height of 4000 feet. The Japanese had occupied the old French outpost at Tam Dao itself, on the crest of the ridge, with forty troops. Giap launched his largest attack up to that time against the post and over-ran the garrison. From the plunder which was taken from the Japanese, Ho and Giap had their first telephone connection between their offices, which were some three hundred yards apart.

The major part of the Viet Minh activities at Tan Trao was preparation for the imminent take-over of the civil administration when the Japanese surrendered. Ho regarded this as his only opportunity to achieve power within the foreseeable future. He knew that the British and Chinese Nationalists were to move into Indo China to take the surrender of the Japanese and to disarm and repatriate them. He also knew that the French would return within months of the ending of the war and that they would be likely to consider negotiations with the Viet Minh only if the latter had already achieved so much strength that they could not be ignored. Consequently the Viet Minh had only a few days in which to make their coup d'état —the time between the Japanese surrender and the arrival of the Allies. Organizational cadres were despatched throughout the length and breadth of Vietnam, so that within a day or two from the given signal, administrations controlled by the Viet Minh could be set up in Hanoi, Hue and Saigon.

The dropping of the atomic bomb on Hiroshima on 7 August 1945 made the immediate end of the war apparent to those most concerned in Vietnam. The Bao Dai government set up under the Japanese resigned that same day, and Ho made ready to launch a general uprising. A national meeting of the Indo China Communist Party assembled at Tan Trao on 13 August, and decided on the same day to issue the call for a nation-wide uprising to take over the government and prepare a welcome for the forces of the Allies. After three days of discussion, another conference was called at Tan Trao, a 'People's Congress' of different political groups and minority groups which formed the 'National Liberation Committee of Vietnam'. This committee was intended to rally political support behind the government which Ho was preparing.

In the meantime, Giap was leading a token military assault on the main Japanese garrison barring the way from the Bac Kan area to Hanoi. While he was at Thai Nguyen, he learned of the call for national uprising and of the initial response in Hanoi, and hastened to assist. After a hard march through the night, spurred on by the thought of the prize of the following day, Giap led his troops into Hanoi. Propaganda leaflets were everywhere, proclaiming the revolution and the Viet Minh as the Vietnamese partner of the Allies who had beaten Japan. Popular support swelled, not specifically for the Viet Minh or for Communism, because few people had any idea that the revolution was Communist organized, but to gain national liberty. On 19 August the Viet Minh took over the public buildings of Hanoi. They sent representatives to talk with Bao Dai in Hue, and the Emperor agreed that Ho Chi Minh should form a government. Popular feeling in Hanoi would not accept a constitution by which Bao Dai remained head of state and so he abdicated on 25 August and left the way open for the introduction of a republican constitution.

While Ho was busy forming his government, the French had lost no time in making contact with the Viet Minh. This suited the Viet Minh because they wished to discover what concessions the French were prepared to consider and Giap was empowered to open the negotiations. Ho had entrusted Giap with the duties of Minister of the Interior and it was in this capacity that he met the newly arrived French Commissioner for North Vietnam, Sainteny, on 27 August. These meetings were inconclusive and they dragged on for several months. However, because neither side was able to open hostilities at this stage, the discussions were treated with respect and Ho himself took part on many occasions.

The abdication of Bao Dai had a crucial effect on the struggle for power in Saigon. After the Japanese surrender, a body known as the United National Front composed of the leading non-Communist political parties took control. These parties, the *Viet Nam Quoc Gia Doc Lap Dang* (Independence Party of Vietnam), the *Thanh Tien Phong* (Vanguard Youth) and the sects, the *Cao Dai* and the *Hoa Hao*, had been associated in the public eye with the Japanese; and Tran Van Giau, Communist Party Commissioner for Cochin China, was quick to stress the point that such a government would be a poor one for negotiations with the Allies. When the people of Saigon heard that Bao Dai had abdicated in favour of the Viet Minh, they felt that he had substantiated the claims of the Viet Minh to be closely associated with the Allies. They began to respond to the pressures of the Communist organizers to demonstrate for a change in government and the United National Front resigned. A massive popular demonstration on 25 August confirmed the strength of the Viet Minh, and Tran Van Giau installed a government which he claimed was the local branch of the Hanoi and Hue governments, the United National Front's gold flag with a red star being replaced by the red flag with a gold star of the Viet Minh.

The northern or main government of Ho Chi Minh was formed on 29 August 1945 and Giap formally became the new Minister of the Interior. This position probably indicates the sort of work which Giap had carried out in addition to his military activities during the previous years. It may well be that these latter duties were much less important than the business of establishing firm control over the people, and that it would be more correct to classify Giap during the years of World War II and afterwards as being fundamentally the controller of the interior, of the political thoughts and actions of the people, with an additional responsibility for the development of an armed force sufficient to enable him to establish control of the internal situation. Until we hear more on this from Giap himself, the situation will remain ambiguous. The important factor to keep in mind is that at no stage did Giap allow his military responsibilities to remove him from the centre of active politics, and his approach to military questions was always that of the politician. Because he was part of politics he never had to worry about observing the limitations governing most other commanders with regard to the supremacy of politics in military affairs. There was no gap between the formulator of military policy for the Viet Minh and the implementer of that policy. Not only could Giap protest more effectively against any military task for which he lacked sufficient means, but he was able to organize backing for those policies which he felt were required by the military situation. Few commanders have ever enjoyed this luxury.

Ho had not established his government any too soon, for in early September British troops began landing in Saigon, followed in October by the French who took control of the South. The Chinese entered Tonkin from the north. The Chinese were accompanied by the remnants of the several Vietnamese parties which had felt unable to re-establish themselves in Vietnam in the face of the Japanese. These nationalists had been most unfortunate in their choice of harbingers, for the Chinese troops behaved abominably as they proceeded overland from the border, helping themselves to whatever they pleased as they advanced. The Chinese presence posed two problems for Ho; first, how to survive the threats to his government which came from the Chinese backed VNQDD, and second, how to get the Chinese out of Vietnam.

The VNQDD under Vu Hong Khanh, and with Chinese assistance, took nominal control of several of the large towns on the Chinese lines of march. The Chinese were not prepared, however, to take the final step and crush Ho in Hanoi. Doubt-less Ho's survival depended greatly on the co-operation he ex-tended towards the Chinese and on the bribes he gave to their commanders, but the Chinese hesitancy to take action against him must also have been due to a reluctance to become in-volved in the fate of Vietnam.

The problem of getting the Chinese to leave was a crucial matter for Ho, because he could not have expected to main-tain his popular support by appearing to act as a puppet of a regime which treated the Vietnamese so harshly. By them-selves, however, the Viet Minh had no hope of expelling the Chinese, and they could look for assistance only from the French, who desired to regain complete control of Indo China. For the Viet Minh, therefore, negotiations had a secret incen-tive after the Chinese arrival. This may also explain why Giap took such great pains to protect the French community in Hanoi from acts of revenge and public brutality during the months after the Japanese surrender.

Giap himself suffered considerably from the activities of the *Dai Viet Quoc Dan Dang*, the *Phuc Quoc Hoi*, and their Chinese supporters, and was kidnapped together with the Propaganda Minister, Tran Huy Lieu, in late 1945. Ho had planned to hold national elections at which he hoped seriously to weaken the opposition parties, and intense negotiations were taking place in Hanoi at that time. One of the conditions Ho had to agree to in order to get his two ministers back was that he would drop them from his government. Ho also agreed that, of the ten seats in the Cabinet, not more than four should be given to his own party.

The Viet Minh, as was to be expected, dominated the other parties in the election results and Giap won 97 per cent of the votes of Nghe An Province. Ho made no haste to admit his opponents to the new national government, preferring to con-duct negotiations with the French and govern with his old team. In January it became clear that the French would be returning to the northern half of Vietnam in the near future and Ho was able to transfer the emphasis of his diplomacy away from the Chinese. In order to give his government the appearance of general support throughout Vietnam, Ho suddenly invited the Nationalists into the cabinet and fulfilled his promise that Giap would be dismissed.

This did not mean political banishment for Giap but rather that the cabinet had ceased to become the most powerful body in Ho's government. Vu Hong Khanh became Defence Minister, but Giap, nominally his deputy, controlled policy matters through the *Quan Su Uy Vien Hoi*, or Committee of Military Commissars. The Defence Ministry merely controlled supplies. Successful compromises were worked out between Ho and the French, chiefly through Commissioner Sainteny, a liberal whose policies were not supported by the French in Saigon or in Paris. The French were to have right of entry for their army into Tonkin until 1952, while the government was to remain in the hands of the Viet Minh. Giap came back into the public arena in support of Ho's policy of conciliation with the French and on 7 March 1946, he skilfully addressed a rally in Hanoi of some 100,000 people who demanded to be told why the French were to be permitted to return. The importance which the Viet Minh attached to good relations with the French while the former were in so weak a position militarily was further emphasized by Giap's speech in praise of the French Army at a joint Franco-Vietnamese military parade held in Hanoi on 22 March.

After the Ho-Sainteny agreement, the Viet Minh pressed the French High Commissioner, Admiral d'Argenlieu, for a full conference in Paris to determine the future of Vietnam. D'Argenlieu could see that Ho would be given a better hearing in Paris than in the colonial atmosphere of Indo China, and he insisted that the conference be held at Dalat. Ho continued to work towards a conference in Paris and finally accepted the Dalat proposal as a preliminary to a higher level meeting.

The Dalat conference assembled on 17 April 1946. Amongst the Vietnamese delegation was Giap, one of the two representatives of the Viet Minh in a group of ten. It soon became apparent that the dominant figure on the Vietnamese side was the former Minister for the Interior. Each side tried hard to preserve an atmosphere of goodwill, and before long the leaders of the French delegation and Giap were addressing each other by the French familiar 'tu'.* The negotiations were carried out both in formal sessions and in informal conversations carried on by groups of twos and threes in the hotel where the conference was held. A French delegate, Bousquet, has written a description of Giap's conduct during a conversation one evening.

> Giap let himself go. . . . Bent forward, with his inscrutable smile, he told us what his youth had been like, how his wife had been imprisoned by the French and had died in jail, his child dead, his life destroyed, and yet, he said, he could wipe all this out and still hold out his hand to us, loyally, swallow his suffering, and reserve his hate for those he considered responsible and whom he did not identify with France.

Bousquet also wrote:

> In the face of his emotion I was somewhat bewildered, but Messmer, calm and imperturbable, answered him. He recalled his odyssey in Tongking several months before, the miles walked through the delta after his arrest, 'speeded on by the force of kicks in the behind', his friend, Captain Brancourt, murdered, and he himself escaping only by a miracle. He added: 'If I remember well, Giap, you were then the Interior Minister.' . . . Giap, whose smile had become somewhat forced, acknowledged the fact. Messmer could therefore say then that he too was without hate, that he too held out his hand, and that all in all, they were more or less even. I observed Giap while Messmer spoke. He was holding a glass in his hand and the glass trembled slightly.[5]

It is significant that these conversations reveal not only desires for compromise and a return to normal relations

---

*The use of 'tu' may have another explanation, for it was commonly used by the French when speaking down to Vietnamese and it was resented. Giap may have tried to equal the score.

[5]Philippe Devillers, *Histoire du Viet-Nam de 1940 a 1952* (Editions du Seuil, Paris, 1952), pp. 263-4. Translated by Joseph Buttinger, *Vietnam: a Dragon Embattled* (Frederick A. Praeger, New York, 1967), p. 643

between the two governments, but they also show the considerable stresses imposed on their dealings by feelings of mutual self-righteousness. The bonds of goodwill were still extremely fragile and susceptible to the injured pride of the two sides. No agreement was reached on fundamental issues, and the French insisted that the Vietnamese wait until the Paris conference for a settlement of disputes regarding sovereignty. Giap was very upset at this outcome, and it is possible that at the Dalat Conference he began to think that war between the French and the Viet Minh was imminent. After his return to Hanoi he threw himself into intense preparations to ensure that if war did come, as he felt it must, the Viet Minh would not be overwhelmed in the first onslaught. The French quickly came to regard Giap as the principal threat to peace in Indo China and claimed to see his hand behind all the moves of the Viet Minh in Hanoi to impede the transfer of sovereignty to the French.

When Ho went off to Paris, he took Pham Van Dong, then Minister of Finance, with him and appointed Giap as head of the government, or *de facto* President, in his absence. A few weeks before Ho's departure the Viet Minh intelligence service had obtained a document prepared within the French High Command ordering local commanders to study measures which might be taken to throw the Viet Minh out of office. With this document it was easy for Giap to further incite the Viet Minh leaders, who felt that they stood in grave danger of a French military offensive and that strenuous measures were needed to preserve their vital interests. Thus the classical pattern of mutual fear and distrust had begun to form and lead towards a pre-emptive strike to start a war which each side thought that it could win.

It was difficult for Giap to envisage how he could defeat the French, in view of their great preponderance of sophisticated weapons and their highly developed economy. Obviously it would be several years at least before he could meet the French Army in a major battle. Therefore the war would be a long one and it would have to be waged on the defensive for some time if the Viet Minh were to survive. Giap had seen from the experience of the Chinese Communists that widespread popular action on a small scale could offset conventional military superiority. He had grown up in the traditions of the Vietnamese struggle against the French, and guerrilla warfare was a subject which he had known as an every day affair during his adolescence and early manhood. Most of the foundations for awakening popular support for a nation wide guerrilla war were already in existence. The French were un-popular, nationalism was a powerful factor in the minds of most Vietnamese, and the Viet Minh had the organization necessary to compel a great proportion of the population to begin fighting for these goals. This political organization needed much expanding and strengthening. However the months of confusion in 1945 had given the Viet Minh such a splendid opportunity for developing a national structure that a French policy of suppression was likely to add more support-ers to the Viet Minh than it removed.

The main problem in Giap's mind in mid 1946 was the method by which the war was to be conducted. Either a national front could be formed which would embrace all of the anti-French parties, or Viet Minh monopoly could be achieved by smashing the non-Communist organizations and intimida-ting their followers. The Indo China Communist Party was in such a position of strength by 1946 that the latter course seemed to Giap to offer the best solution, and he exploited his power during Ho's absence to break the power of the non-Communist parties. He went about this design with a degree of subtlety, attempting to coerce all Vietnamese parties into a front called the *Lien Viet* or Popular National Front. Of course all power within this front was held by the Viet Minh but any party which refused to join and to submit to its auth-ority was publicly branded as reactionary and treacherous and was dealt with accordingly by the terrorist teams of the government.

The 1946 campaign for national solidarity behind the *Lien Viet* gave Giap an opportunity for striking down the strongest

opposition groups—the VNQDD and the *Dai Viet*. Both
parties realized what the *Lien Viet* implied for their future, and
both endeavoured to oppose it. Unfortunately for them, they
had no political programme which could hope to counter that
of the Viet Minh, and their leadership was not of sufficient
standard to appear even as a feasible alternative to Ho, Dong
and Giap. The only point on which the Viet Minh were seriously vulnerable was their policy of co-operation with the
French, for not only did many Vietnamese feel that this concession was too much to be stomached; it also appeared to
prejudice the entire movement for national independence.
Consequently the VNQDD foolishly succumbed to the temptation to discredit the Viet Minh in the eyes of the people as
lackeys of the French, and they also attempted to provoke
clashes between the two.

The end of the VNQDD was predictably swift and brutal.
As soon as the last Chinese Nationalist troops had withdrawn
in June 1946, the Viet Minh disbanded the troublesome party,
killing many of its leaders and throwing out of office all those
local governments which had been under their control. By
July some unprincipled elements of the VNQDD had thrown
their lot in with the *Lien Viet* and a new, reformed VNQDD
was founded by the Viet Minh.

Other unco-operative parties such as the *Dai Viet* and the
adherents to the *Dong Minh Hoi* met similar fates and their
last members were rounded up in a series of military pursuits
conducted by the Viet Minh, often extending as far as the
Tonkinese border regions. A number of purges of government
officials and of lower echelons of the Party were carried out by
the Viet Minh, and their opponents quickly discovered the
virtues of discretion. During the months of Ho's absence, Giap
was responsible for the deaths of hundreds of his political
opponents, for the destruction of any apparatus capable of
rivalling the Viet Minh, and for the suppression of all newspapers which were not under the control of his government. He
also built up the strength of the Viet Minh Army from 30,000
to 60,000 and formed many irregular units such as the *Tu Ve*

which could submerge themselves amongst the civilians with whom they lived, emerging only for brief intervals to carry out military operations.

After the suppression of the VNQDD and the *Dai Viet*, the need for close Franco-Viet Minh co-operation decreased from the points of view of both sides, and a number of incidents involving the forces of one or the other or both occurred. The most serious clash was at Bac Ninh, thirteen miles north east of Hanoi, on 2 August 1946, when some Viet Minh ambushed a French convoy. The French brought in aircraft and artillery, and a settlement with the local Viet Minh was swiftly reached.

During this difficult year, Giap re-married. His private life between 1940 and 1945 is completely unknown, but from what is known of the periods before and after this interval, it would seem foolish to suggest that it did not exist. In 1946, the affections of many young North Vietnamese had become focused on a striking and beautiful singer of sad songs, Thuong Huyen. Whatever people may have thought about the occasional connection of the names of Giap and Thuong Huyen, a wave of disapproval arose when it was apparent that Giap had more ambitious intentions. Was this a further manifestation of Giap's bourgeois nature, many wondered, harking back to his image of 1945 when his favourite garb had been a white duck suit, a club stripe tie and a trilby hat. Even if Giap was not abusing the ideological privileges of his position, it appeared to many that he was certainly exploiting his social position beyond reasonable bounds.

The conference at Fontainebleau achieved little more than its predecessor at Dalat. Ho returned to Hanoi in October 1946 bearing only a *modus vivendi* as fruit of his conciliatory policy towards the French and he had many difficulties in containing the frustration of his more radical supporters, who clamoured for an end to co-operation with the colonialists. A new government was formed on 3 November with increased Communist control and elimination of all real opponents. Five out of ten cabinet places went to openly avowed Communists, and the remaining ministries went to members of parties which were under Viet Minh control. This new government enabled Giap to return to an official position as Minister of National Defence. It is interesting that his portfolio was not that of the Interior; clearly, times were changing, and military security was going to be of greater importance to the Viet Minh than the internal political contest. In one way, it may be said that with five seats in the Cabinet, the Viet Minh had no need to concern themselves with internal politics beyond maintaining the strength of their own organization throughout the country: this was hardly a cabinet matter.

The new Assembly which had been elected in October proceeded to approve a new constitution which, on 8 November, established the Democratic Republic of Vietnam. The Assembly also elected a Permanent Committee to carry on the crucial functions of government, including the voting of government bills, and granted the Permanent Committee the powers to declare a state of war and to summon the Assembly. On 14 November 1946 the Assembly went into abeyance and was not recalled to session until December 1953.

During the last months of 1946, Tonkin became the scene of an arms race. The Viet Minh organized a supply of former Chinese weapons brought in by both road and sea, and the French began to increase their garrisons. The point of entry for most of the arms of both sides was the port of Haiphong, and this city soon became the centre of the worst Franco-Vietnamese crisis of 1945 and 1946. The French knew that the Viet Minh were using Haiphong for arms shipments and they began to edge the Communists out of local control. The Viet Minh fully appreciated the significance of these attempts and dug their heels in. French troops expelled the Viet Minh from the Customs House in August 1946, and the joint intervention of Giap and General Morlière, the French commander in Tonkin, was necessary to restore peace. The French gave the Viet Minh an ultimatum to hand over complete control of the customs at Haiphong by 15 October. The Viet Minh realized that in view of the significance of Haiphong this ultimatum amounted to a threat of war, and they protested to

Paris. No answer was received from France and each side continued to make frantic preparations for the conflict which now
seemed inevitable.

Tension continued to mount through the first weeks of
November to such a level that one incident would be sufficient
to lead to general hostilities and war between the French and
the Viet Minh. This incident came on 20 November. The
French seized a Chinese junk suspected of carrying arms for
the Viet Minh. The Viet Minh captured three French soldiers
and barricaded their part of the town. The French tore down
the barricades and some heavy fighting took place. A conference in Hanoi agreed on terms for a cease-fire which went
into effect at 5 p.m. on 21 November. However, the French
High Command in Saigon did not want a cease fire, and the
local commander was ordered to submit to the Viet Minh an
ultimatum as intolerable as that which the Austrians delivered
to the Serbs in 1914. This policy had been sanctioned by both
the Governor General, d'Argenlieu, and the Prime Minister,
Bidault. On the refusal of the Viet Minh to quit Haiphong on
23 November, the French bombarded the Vietnamese part of
Haiphong with the cruiser *Suffren*, with tanks, artillery and aircraft. No one can say for certain how many Vietnamese were
killed that day—the Viet Minh claim 20,000 and the French
6,000—but this bombardment had shown the Viet Minh that
henceforward the problems of local power could be resolved
only by force.

Once the French had reached this point, any desire for
moderation appears to have left them, and another ultimatum
was issued, this time to the government in Hanoi, demanding
complete control over Hanoi and the road to Haiphong. The
Viet Minh were clever enough to see that the French were
merely trying to goad them into aggression and for this reason
the Viet Minh were resolved to act with great restraint and
thereby avoid the charge of belligerence. This policy must have
paid off handsomely in terms of popular support during the
difficult years ahead.

Giap responded by sending the greater part of the main

forces to the northern provinces of Bac Kan, Tuyen Quang
and Thai Nguyen, the southern part of the Viet Bac where
Giap and Ho had established their movement in the early
'forties. Responsibility for local security in the towns and
villages was given to the *Tu Ve*. Barricades sprang up in the
Hanoi streets and small clashes occurred. The French dealt
with these by severe reprisals against the neighbourhood in
which these incidents took place.

Ho appealed to the French government in Paris for moderation of the demands which had been placed on him and offered
continued co-operation in the spirit of the *modus vivendi* of the
previous September. He knew that Admiral d'Argenlieu was
to be replaced and so he had some grounds to hope for a
peaceful future, provided that the local French commanders
did not press their demands too hard and that Ho was able to
control the hotheads amongst his own followers. The situation
in Hanoi reached the point of explosion on the morning of 19
December 1946, when the French insisted that the *Tu Ve* be
disarmed as proof of the Viet Minh's peaceful intentions. The
Vietnamese obstructed the streets and the French then took
over control of the traffic police. Giap saw General Morlière during the afternoon and asked him to allow his troops
out of their barrack confinement as a means of reducing tension. Morlière agreed to this and French soldiers were soon in
the streets, cafes, bars and cinemas.

At 6.30 p.m. Morlière received a report from an agent that
Giap was planning an attack with the *Tu Ve*, and the French
soldiers were called back from leave to their barracks. Whether
Giap was actually planning an attack is not known, but several
accounts by Vietnamese who were in Hanoi at this time suggest that a Viet Minh strike was expected. However the Viet
Minh had much to gain by biding their time, and they certainly
had insufficient troops and weapons to oust the French from
Hanoi at that time. All that can be said is that the *Tu Ve*
attacked the French garrisons at 8 p.m. and that Giap issued
a national call to arms at 9.30 p.m. Possibly the French recall
of their troops provoked some impatient *Tu Ve* leaders to

make a pre-emptive strike. If this attack is seen as part of Giap's plan, it seems surprising that there was such a lag between the commencement of fighting and Giap's message to the nation. Further speculation about the immediate causes of the fighting of 19 December 1946 seems fruitless in view of the general atmosphere of tension and of the events in Haiphong during the previous month. Unless much more caution had been shown by both sides in Hanoi, the outbreak of open hostilities was merely a matter of time.

Savage fighting lasted for several days in Hanoi and protracted resistance went on all through January 1947. The Viet Minh leaders fled to the Viet Bac, and uprisings began at many points throughout Vietnam. The French had the better of the Viet Minh in the towns and expelled them into the wilder regions of the country. Unfortunately for the French, so much of Vietnam is covered by jungles and rugged mountains that this action achieved little. While they had been in the towns, the Viet Minh had at least been subject to French observation and the French knew where to find them; once the Viet Minh had taken to the jungles, they were almost completely beyond the reach of the French intelligence system, and the environment protected them from pursuit. By the end of March 1947 the French had taken control of the major coastal and delta towns in Tonkin and northern Annam, and of the roads between them. Giap had chosen to preserve his slender forces so that they could be trained and expanded in the security of the Viet Bac until they had reached sufficient strength to emerge and challenge the French to fight for their cheap gains of early 1947.

During the first months of consolidation in the Viet Bac, Ho Chi Minh attempted to improve his position by bringing more of the non-Communist nationalists into the struggle against the French. Ho could do this only by appearing to be somewhat less Communist and more nationalist, and the obvious starting point was to get rid of Giap, the man who was irrevocably associated in the popular mind with the reign of terror which had tightened the Viet Minh grip on Tonkin

during the absence of Ho in 1946. When it seemed possible
that even Bao Dai might throw his support behind the Viet
Minh, Ho did not shrink from acting, and in July 1947 he
formed a new cabinet which gave more representation, but not
more power, to the non-Communists, and which contained
neither Giap nor Pham Van Dong. Despite their absence from
the cabinet, both Giap and Dong continued to exert a powerful influence through their closeness to Ho and through Giap's
undisputed control of the armed forces.

The rapid expansion of French military control throughout
the countryside had contributed appreciably to French
vulnerability, for they lacked sufficient strength to hold most
of the towns of Vietnam and at the same time to concentrate
their forces to repel the attacks which the Viet Minh were
capable of launching. Although the French might have a
garrison of, say, company strength in a village, sufficient to
maintain control over the surrounding countryside by day, this
outpost could fall to a battalion attack in the hours of dark-
ness. The small patrols with which the French cleared the
ground between the strongpoints could be ambushed by Viet
Minh in superior numbers from time to time, since Viet Minh
troops were not spread so thinly on the ground. Giap ordered
his guerrilla commands to exploit their ability to concentrate
locally superior forces for a short time in order to continually
harass and wear down the French. Roads and bridges were
blown up and when they were repaired, they were blown up
again. When the French came in strength to look for their
tormentors, the Viet Minh dispersed into the huge areas of
jungle and eluded pursuit. Soon the French realized that they
could control only a small amount of Vietnam, less than half
of the country by day and less than a quarter by night. In view
of the serious economic and military weaknesses of France
after World War II, the French Army in 1947 was in an
extremely unfavourable position to attempt the defeat of the
Viet Minh, even in a military sense.

However, the French High Command did not view the situation so pessimistically and the Commander in Chief,

General Valluy, began to plan an offensive aimed at striking deep into the Viet Bac and at wiping out the vital leadership of the Viet Minh. Valluy's aim was at least bold enough to go to the heart of the trouble, and he must be given credit for insight into the difficulties which would arise for the French if the war became a protracted, inconclusive war of attrition. However, the boldness of his aim required Valluy to take particular care in planning the details of his operation, for if he missed capturing Ho at the first attempt, he was not likely to be given a second chance.

The area which Ho and Giap had picked for their main base was roughly circular in shape, with a fifty mile radius, centred approximately on Bac Kan which was over eighty miles north of Hanoi. The region was deeply dissected by steep valleys between the high ridges which ran down to the south-east from Yunnan towards the Gulf of Tonkin. These ridges, forming a knotted tangle, with only vague suggestions of general regularity, were very different from the straight spines which occur in Western Tonkin. Varying in height from two to four thousand feet, they were composed of limestone Karst, honeycombed with caves which provided refuge from pursuit and from air attack. The Viet Bac has an eighty inch annual rainfall, three quarters of which falls between the months of May and November, offering a protective blanket of moisture and fog for six months of the year. To mount offensive operations on a large scale during the south-west monsoon was almost impossible for an army which depended to any extent on mechanical transport and air power. Once May 1947 had passed without a French attack in the Viet Bac, Giap was able to be almost certain that he had another five months for preparations before he had to worry greatly about Valluy's intentions.

The ruggedness of the country and the high rainfall had combined to make movement very difficult, except by foot. Roads and bridges were few while streams and rivers abounded. Foot tracks used by the local inhabitants linked each settlement with several others, but there were almost no roads which could take wheeled vehicles (apart from ox carts). The only road which crossed the region was Route 3 which ran from Thai Nguyen through Bac Kan to Cao Bang. For most of its length, Route 3 was no better than a cart track, winding through narrow valleys which could be dominated by a small ambush party firing down on the heads of men on the road from invisible and inaccessible positions. Route 4 ran along the north-eastern edge, linking Lang Son, That Khe, Dong Khe and Cao Bang, while Route 2 went around the western edge through Tuyen Quang to Ha Giang close to the Yunnan border. The only river system which offered access into the region for moderate sized boats and landing craft was the Clear River and its tributary, the Song Gam.

The French could not see many feasible alternatives for crushing Giap's forces in the Viet Bac. The area was too large for a cordon to be placed around it and a systematic search made, so that the only way of penetrating it was to make several deep thrusts along suitable lines of approach. When one looked at the question of what might for French purposes be considered a suitable line of approach, again the answers were disappointingly few. If the French were not to fight with equipment, supplies and transport on a level with those of the guerrillas they were chasing, they had to depend on Route 3, Route 4 and the Clear River–Song Gam system. Thus the Viet Minh could afford to concentrate their defences on a few lines of approach only, and they felt that they would have ample warning of a French thrust by virtue of the great depth of the area in which they were based. Once the alert had been given, there were many suitable refuge areas to which an army which did not wish to be brought to battle could flee with small risk of pursuit.

Valluy was quite determined to make an all-out effort to put a finish to the Viet Minh in 1947. He knew that they would not be welcome in Nationalist China, so for as long as Chiang Kai-shek remained in power, the French might expect Ho Chi Minh to be on their side of the border. However, the state of affairs in China looked far from hopeful for the Nationalist government, and the day when Ho Chi Minh could supply his forces directly from a Communist China seemed to Valluy to be much too close to be ignored.

The French commander's appreciation of the problems of this offensive, *Operation Lea*, recognized that the only land routes into the Bac Kan area were via Routes 3 and 4 and the Clear River–Song Gam, and he proposed that two arms of a pincer movement should use them, while an airborne force would be dropped into Bac Kan itself at the same time as the land forces set out, so that Ho would not have sufficient warning to escape. Valluy was under considerable pressure to carry out a major operation which might yield a notable success, because the French Chamber of Deputies was becoming reluctant to vote the funds necessary for the continuance of the war, and because a rebellion on Madagascar threatened to take·15,000 of Valluy's reserves from him. The French government had gone so far as to promise to reduce the number of troops in Indo China from 115,000 to 90,000, so that Valluy was being forced to disregard whatever reservations he may have had about attempting such an ambitious offensive.

The extent of the French commitment in the form of small garrisons dotted about the length and breadth of Indo China meant that Valluy had only a very limited force at his disposal: three battalions of armoured vehicles, six of infantry, two of paratroops, four of artillery and one of engineers, the Fourth Fighter Group of the French Air Force, and a small fleet of tank landing craft of the French Navy. Together with supporting units, this force totalled some 15,000 men. Its task was to find and defeat a force of 60,000 in an area of 7,500 square miles of jungle-covered peaks. By the standards of more recent operations in Vietnam, a reasonable task for such a force would have been to defeat a force of 3,000 guerrillas within an area of 400 square miles. Whatever the French may have lacked in their operational thinking, it was certainly not the spirit of boldness.

The various political pressures on Valluy are not sufficient to explain this amazing disparity between his means and his goal. His intelligence estimates of Viet Minh strength at this time held that Giap had only a few thousand poorly equipped and trained irregulars whose will to resist might be easily broken once they had seen that their base areas were not secure from French offensives. Also it must be remembered that this operation was the first large scale assault ever to be undertaken against the Viet Minh and that French forces had not fought through this area since the late nineteenth century. In view of his training and experience of conventional warfare in Europe, Valluy probably had no idea of the enormous numbers of men needed to cordon off an area of Vietnamese jungle. In thick country, a battalion of infantry cannot guarantee to close off more than one mile of frontage. Valluy's ten battalions of infantry and armour backed up by the garrisons scattered around the edges of the Viet Bac area were required to close off a frontage of over three hundred miles if the Viet Minh were to be prevented from slipping through the French net. Another factor working against the French was the classical disadvantage of operating on exterior lines. Giap's forces were within a short distance of their supply bases and he could move them from one front to another on radial routes which passed through the supply centres. Had Valluy wished to redispose his forces from one arm of the pincer to the other, he would have had to send his men on long journeys around the periphery of the Viet Bac.

The final French operational plan assigned three infantry, three armoured and three artillery battalions to the northern pincer which was to set out from Lang Son, proceed up Route 4 to Cao Bang, eighty miles to the north-west, veer west to Nguyen Binh, and then south for forty miles along Route 3 to Bac Kan. The southern pincer consisted of three infantry battalions carried in the naval landing craft up the Clear River to its junction with the Song Gam, and then up the Song Gam for as far as river conditions permitted—probably for some forty miles into Viet Minh controlled territory. These two pincers failed to meet by forty miles and this gap was to be closed by the two battalions which made up the airborne half-brigade which was to parachute into the central area, as close to Ho's headquarters as possible, and conduct a defensive battle, holding the Viet Minh troops in order to crush them with the two arms of the pincer.

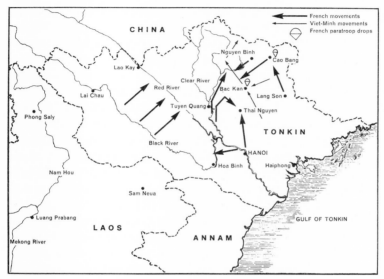

The French Offensive, 1947

Operation Lea was launched on 7 October 1947 with the commencement of the northern thrust and the dropping of some 1,100 paratroops over Bac Kan, Cho Don and Cho Moi, a triangular area twenty miles by ten. The southern drive up the river system began two days later. The near success of the paratroops indicates that Giap was not fully prepared for so ambitious an offensive against his forces. He has since told of how he and Ho Chi Minh had to flee at such short notice that they could only jump into a hole which had been prepared as an emergency hide, relying on good camouflage to elude the French troops who were beating the bush within yards of where they were crouched.[6] Once the first French sweep had

⁶J. R. Tournoux, *Secrets d' état* (Plon, Paris, 1960), p. 11

passed by, the Viet Minh leaders were able to slip away to an area beyond the reach of the two French battalions and to direct the battle which was beginning as the heavily superior numbers of the Viet Minh forces were arrayed around the 1,100 Frenchmen. The situation of these paratroops soon became desperate, since the relief of the northern pincer was still several days away.

Giap then attempted to slow down the northern force by ordering massive demolitions along Routes 3 and 4, making the French engineers the chief controllers of the rate of advance. Nothing which Giap could do could entirely prevent the French from rebuilding the road and the bridges as they worked their way forward under the weight of artillery barrages and air strikes which the Viet Minh could not counter. After several days, it became clear to Giap that the northern pincer looked like winning through before his force at Bac Kan had overrun the paratroop defences. He ordered a last ditch stand to be made by the unit holding the road junction of Phu Tong Hoa, ten miles north of Bac Kan in the narrow valley of the Phu Tan River, along which Route 3 wound its way south. After three days of severe fighting, the motorized Moroccan Colonial Infantry Regiment broke through to relieve the exhausted paratroops on 16 October.

The progress of the southern thrust had been disappointingly slow. The rivers were much more difficult to navigate than had been anticipated because of sand bars. One battalion had to be off-loaded at Tuyen Quang and the remainder of the force had just reached Chiem Hoa on 19 October to find that the northern and central groups were emerging from the mountains to meet them. The operation was continued until 8 November but the small numbers of French troops were unable to prevent the Viet Minh from filtering through the loose cordon to escape to other hiding places which Giap had the foresight to prepare, fifty miles away in the mountains. To have maintained a pursuit would have called for a French effort far greater than the one from which they were by now recovering, so that Valluy could do little but call off the operation and be content with what limited success had been achieved.

At the end of November he began another sweep, *Operation Ceinture*, directed against the Viet Minh on the southern fringe of the Viet Bac, the area from which attacks against the French positions in the Red River Delta could be mounted most easily. The two most important towns of the area, Tuyen Quang and Thai Nguyen, were under an appreciable degree of Viet Minh control and Valluy wished to crush the main force units which were preventing the French from establishing their rule. *Operation Ceinture* was mounted with approximately the same number of troops as *Operation Lea* but the area to be covered was only fifty miles by thirty. Two of the best Viet Minh regiments were based here and the French were able to force them out and capture large amounts of carefully gathered supplies. However, the enemy troops evaded a major battle and the regiments remained intact to infiltrate back into their old domain after the French had withdrawn on 22 December 1947.

The effectiveness of indigenous troops in Vietnam was demonstrated clearly by a third operation launched by the French in 1947. Two battalions of T'ai mountain tribesmen under French officers swept the Viet Minh out of the mountains between the Red and Black rivers with such effectiveness that the Viet Minh were unable to use the area for major operations until 1952. These battalions lived in their area of operations and they fought with the same methods as the Viet Minh, whom they hated, living off the countryside and receiving reliable intelligence reports from their kinsfolk whenever the Viet Minh attempted to move against them.

The French High Command claimed to have killed 9,500 Viet Minh on these operations. If this figure is correct, then it was a worthwhile gain for the employment of 15,000 troops for two months. However, in terms of the over-all strategic balance, if this was the worst that the French could do to the

Viet Minh while the latter were in their defensive phase, then the outlook for the following years appeared gloomy for the French.

Giap's response was to disperse his forces over a wider area, in case the French repeated their efforts to smash his embryo force, and to step up his efforts to tie the French down throughout Vietnam. Both these purposes were served by the creation of independent companies, formed from part of the regular army and sent deep into all French-held areas with the double task of waging the propaganda war for the allegiance of the people and of carrying on guerrilla activities against the French. Ho was quick to see the wisdom of Giap's suggestion and approved it while the fighting around Bac Kan was at its height.

The French presence in northern Tonkin was brief and restricted. After the cessation of major operations on 22 December 1947 the French withdrew to the delta, to the coastal plain which ran up to the Chinese border from Haiphong, and to the chain of forts they had established along Route 4 between Lang Son and Cao Bang. Although these forts were strung out in a thin line to which access was possible only from one end, Valluy was convinced that some action had to be taken to prevent Ho Chi Minh from using China as a sanctuary and a source of supplies. Alas for the French Army —there were so many points which had become 'vital' to the security of French rule that the Army was spread too thinly over the country to be able to cope with the local concentrations which Viet Minh strength permitted.

By 1948, then, Giap was beginning to see that there were reasonable hopes that the French could be restricted to a small part of Vietnam, and that if he maintained all-round pressure, they could be kept so spread out that they could be defeated in detail by skilful use of troops whose equipment and firepower were not equal to winning a pitched battle against a large formation. He knew that the French could not eject him from the Viet Bac and so there was no need for his preparations for taking the war to the French to be hastened beyond the point of maximum efficiency. In other words, the French inability to crush Giap in the Viet Bac had left the initiative open to him. Once he attacked, the French would have to respond. It now remained for him to plan his attack so that the French response would cost them the heaviest losses.

Despite the Viet Minh misfortunes of the two years after World War II, they had managed to survive the French return and to keep the major part of their armed forces intact. They controlled more of the country than the French and they had been able to undercut their domestic political opposition so effectively that they had become the only feasible rallying point for nationalist feeling against the French. The conservative ideas of the colonial power, and the heavy-handedness of the French Army, had made powerful contributions to the numbers who were prepared to support the Viet Minh in their efforts to win independence, and these numbers appeared to be continually increasing. Events of 1947 had shown that December 1946 had been the low point of Viet Minh fortunes. Giap's basis for planning a protracted war was sound, and the portents indicated that it would become stronger unless the French were prepared to sacrifice part of their war aims and grant a moderate degree of independence to the political opponents of the Viet Minh. Yet even this threat could be countered by expert use of a reliable weapon—terror.

These two years had seen a corresponding improvement in the position of Giap. He had become somewhat of an object of barter in internal politics, but this was merely a superficial transaction. His selection as head of the government during the absence of Ho and Dong in Paris has shown beyond all doubt that Giap was third ranking in the hierarchy of the Communist Party, and that he was quite capable of running the affairs of the nation for a lengthy period. In other words, he was of presidential calibre. However, he had exercised power at a difficult time, when it had been necessary for the sake of Viet Minh control to repress some of his compatriots; and he had become marked as an extremist, a label which Ho was doubtless thankful to avoid through his absence in Paris. In the military sphere, Giap had learned that he could survive the best efforts of the French, provided that he employed moderate caution. He had been able to elude the French Army's attempts to force him into a decisive battle and this had given him sufficient lee-way to take the initiative into his own hands with leisurely deliberation. He was now receiving a general's training and a general's experience.

4 Winning the Initiative

The French withdrawal from the mountains of the Viet Bac in late 1947 may have been necessary to meet the short term requirements of the French Army but it gave the Viet Minh a vital respite, sufficient to allow them to develop an overwhelming strength. The French commander, General Valluy, did not entirely abandon the mountains, for he maintained a garrison at Bac Kan itself until, by August 1948, the road from Cao Bang along which supplies came had become too difficult to use. However, this garrison was unable to do more than to hold a bridgehead for possible future operations and the Viet Minh simply walked around it whenever it lay on their route from one area to another. Apart from the Red River delta, the French had only two other areas from which they could threaten the Viet Bac—the chain of forts along the Chinese border from Lang Son to Cao Bang and the mountain town of Ha Giang, situated in the Clear River Valley close to the Chinese border, eighty miles west of Cao Bang. Provided that Giap kept a close watch on these two points and along the northern edge of the Red River delta, he had ample warning of any French trespass into his hundred mile wide domain of tangled hills, rivers and jungles.

In effect, Giap now had a military sabbatical year in which he thought out the nature of the war which lay ahead, and the strategic tools which might be necessary, and began to build the forces which the nature of the war demanded. The principles of Mao Tse-tung, which Giap had absorbed during the years of World War II, formed the basis for Viet Minh military policy. There were many similarities between Vietnam in 1948 and China in 1936, including a semi-colonial state of development, a Communist leadership which could command the support of large sections of the population, the presence of a powerful hostile army, and the relative weakness of the Communist forces. These essential characteristics of all revolutionary war, according to Mao, indicated that victory could not be won by the Communists quickly. They would have to wait patiently until the strength of popular support and the ruggedness of the country had combined to offset the power of the enemy sufficiently to permit the Communist main forces to begin a final offensive phase. Giap has shown in his writings that he had appreciated that the war would have to be waged over several years, and hence immediate operational plans had no particular urgency. It is rare that a field commander can take this sort of leisurely approach, and when he is as intelligent as Giap, he is likely to derive considerable advantage from taking his time.

According to the three classical phases of revolutionary war, the Viet Minh had to pass from the strategic defensive through guerrilla warfare to the counter-offensive. In 1947, they had clearly been in the first stage, and the launching of the second was yet to be planned. While the second stage was in progress, the third stage had to be prepared for by training large forces who would be used to fight the conventional battles which would drive the enemy, it was hoped, into the sea. Because the conduct of warfare at the local guerrilla level calls for political more than military effort, in raising bands of young men and in persuading the population that they ought to support these bands, Giap declared that political activities were to take precedence over military tasks. In essence, this concept meant that if an action, for example an ambush, could cause political harm through killing some Vietnamese civilians as well as some French soldiers, it was not to be attempted. The support of the civilians would be of more use against the French in the future than the loss of a few French soldiers would be of harm to the latter.

In forming this policy, Giap capitalized on the advantage he had over the French, who served for short periods only in Indo China. His troops were there for the rest of their lives and could afford to be certain of success before they acted. The French soldiers, entering a situation which was known to be bad, were anxious to achieve a military improvement within periods of a few months. This pressing urgency, caused partly by fear of a political collapse in Paris, inclined the French to ignore popular opinion amongst the Vietnamese and to concentrate on killing Viet Minh. Admittedly the French had little to offer the Vietnamese people; but to ignore the people while the Viet Minh made great efforts to win their minds was to create far more potential enemies than the Expeditionary Corps could ever defeat. Giap showed the benefits he had derived from his earlier political training, particularly in the propaganda field, in realizing that military might was but one type of power amongst many others, and that the basis of military strength was political strength. In a short war, military acts which erode the basis of political support—such as failure to administer those civilians caught in the theatre of war—may be tolerable in terms of the overall result: in a protracted war, the ultimate strength is the political will of the entire nation, and any loss of political strength represents an equal or greater loss of military strength.

The proper conclusion for the French High Command to have drawn after the failure of Valluy's offensives of 1947 was not that the Viet Minh ought to be fought by military means on ground of French choice, but that the French had somehow to capture a greater part of the popular affection than the Viet Minh could. Unless this was achieved, the whole of the war effort would have to be borne by the populations of France, her allies, and her dependants. The incentives for these people to carry on the war would be insufficient to maintain the effort, as a modicum of political realism might show, and so the whole French effort would go for nothing.

While these thoughts were escaping the attention of French leaders, they did not elude the Viet Minh. Perhaps it was a little easier for Giap than for Valluy, for the former had no outside base of support to which he could look in order to sustain the main war effort. Giap's thoughts could not be distracted from his immediate problems by a feeling that other great powers would not let him go under if the worst happened. He ordered that all troops should take a ten point oath, which he had composed himself during World War II, and which included the following as point 9:

> In contacts with the people, to follow these three recommendations:
> to respect the people
> to help the people
> to defend the people . . . in order to win their confidence and affection and achieve a perfect understanding between the people and the army.[7]

These thoughts were carried into practice through organized days of army assistance to villagers with rice growing, flood control and drought amelioration. In contrast to the soldiers of the Chinese Nationalists and some of the Vietnamese units who fought for the French, the soldiers of the Viet Minh were strictly forbidden to help themselves to food, shelter, material goods and female companionship which did not belong to them.

The winning of popular support, and the relation of Mao's doctrines to the Vietnamese situation, were the two main strategic concerns of Giap in 1948 and 1949. Apart from the strategic problems of the highest level, Giap was also responsible for the training of the army, and much of his thought went on the normal problems of tactics which exercise the

---

[7]Vo Nguyen Giap, *People's War People's Army* (Foreign Languages Publishing House, Hanoi, 1961; p. 56 (Frederick A. Praeger, New York, 1962).

mind of any competent commander. While these questions were of great importance, they are not sufficiently unusual to require special comment. In dealing with them, Giap showed that in addition to being a strategist and a political thinker, he was also a tactician of the first rank. His experience during World War II had given him sufficient grasp of the problems of command on the lower levels to ensure that his higher level planning was based on practical realities and observed the physical limitations which can so easily escape any commander who allows himself to get out of touch with the problems which his troops continually have to face.

In 1950, Giap published a short book, *The War of Liberation and the Popular Army*, setting forth what special military doctrine Viet Minh experience had shown to be useful. He stressed the notion of protracted war and the need for sound minor tactics, and pointed to lack of Viet Minh success in the south as evidence of lack of political training. His concept of the most urgent of the problems confronting him in 1948 becomes clear when he refers to this period as the commencement of the second phase of the revolutionary war. Guerrilla activity and propaganda spreading were the vital elements of this phase while the more classical strategic problems associated with the war of movement demanded by the third phase were only just beginning to turn over in his mind.

Giap was not the only strategist amongst the Viet Minh higher echelons, for Truong Chinh had also been thinking and writing about these problems. His thoughts have been collected in *Primer for Revolt: The Communist Takeover in Vietnam*, a volume which appeared before Giap's. There have been persistent reports of rivalry between Giap and Truong Chinh, and this may explain the reason for two works on similar problems being made public at the same time. Truong Chinh's ideas are generally more extreme than those of Giap and he goes into greater detail on the lower level type of operation. However, the vital concepts of the political dependence of the army on the people have had their best expansion by Giap, and it is possibly through his political outlook on all facets of

war that Giap has managed to prevent control of the Viet
Minh, and later the North Vietnamese military forces, from
falling into the hands of Truong Chinh.

The years of 1948 and 1949 were also important for the
development of the Viet Minh organization. The three classes
of military force—local guerrillas, regional troops, and regulars—who formed the core of the Viet Minh striking power,
were thoroughly overhauled and trained. Men who proved
themselves proficient as guerrillas were advanced to the regional units, and a few of these were taken into the main force as
regulars, to leaven the new recruits. In this way, the size of
the regular component was steadily increased. In April 1949
Giap commanded 32 regular and 137 regional battalions,
while in June 1951 he had 117 regular battalions and 37 of
regional troops.

Political supremacy was maintained by raising the status of
political officers attached to units to a level at which they could
overrule a military commander with whom they differed. These
political officers were controlled by the Party through the
Political Bureau of the Ministry of Defence, which commanded both the regular divisions and the territorial regions.
Their control went right down to units as small as companies,
below which level political supervision was carried out by
Party cells of squad size. Viet Minh soldiers were almost never
split into groups of less than three, and no man knew when
one of his cell colleagues would report him to a political officer
for lack of political ardour. These cells were supposed to meet
formally at frequent intervals, even daily, for mutual discussion and self-criticism. With these command techniques, Giap
obviously had no problems of disobedience, not only with
regard to a specific order but also to general tactical and
strategic notions.

During 1948 and 1949, Giap had restricted the size of his
regular units to regiments of approximately 2,000 men. The
chief factor limiting the further expansion of his largest units
was the problem of providing adequate support, both logistical
and tactical. There were not the resources available for supply-

ing divisional sized units of 10,000 men with food, clothing and ammunition necessary to provide that additional degree of initiative which justifies such large formations. Nor were there sufficient guns and heavy weapons to make up a divisional type of organization. Certainly Giap could group a number of regiments together to make up the numbers required for several divisions, but these groupings could not be assigned the tactical role of a division without the fire support needed to offset the risks incurred in concentrating such a large number of men for an operation.

The military command structure which came into effect in March 1948 divided the nation into six 'integrated zones', usually referred to as interzones. The notion of integration was derived from the composition of the controlling bodies of each zone, which combined political and military leaders, both local representatives and nominees of Viet Minh headquarters in the Viet Bac. Beneath these interzones were interprovinces and intervillages. The interzones (*Lien Khu*) covered the following areas: i. North-west Tonkin; ii. North-east Tonkin; iii. the Red River delta; iv. Annam from Quang Tri Province northward; v. Southern Annam; vi. Cochin China. For military purposes, the country was further subdivided into free zones (Viet Bac; the estuaries of Northern Annam—Thanh Hoa, Nghe An and Ha Tinh; the coast south of Hue—Quang Nam, Quang Ngai and Binh Dinh; the Plain of Reeds; and the Transbassac in the extreme south), guerrilla zones (principally the deltas of the Mekong and the Red Rivers, the central Annamese coast and the Central Mountain Plateau), guerrilla bases which lay close to the guerrilla areas (including War Zones C and D near Saigon), and occupied areas (including Hanoi, Saigon, Hue, Nam Dinh, Haiphong, Hongay, the rubber plantations in Cochin China and the lower Mekong).

Despite this well organized system, the headquarters in the North had considerable difficulty in controlling affairs in the South. The land journey was too long and hazardous for frequent contacts to be made between the leadership in each area, and the only alternative means was by radio. Talking at a distance of several hundred miles was a poor substitute for the sort of direct personal contact through tightly controlled committees which were the backbone of the Viet Minh administration in the North. The inability of the North to contribute any assistance to the weaker movement in the South also gave the Southerners a great deal of autonomy, and one of the principal means for coercion by the North was thereby absent. Indeed, the situation was reversed, for the South made small contributions to the North, and although these were not vital, they did give the Southern leaders a certain leverage with the headquarters in the Viet Bac. This relationship was aggravated by the normal attitudes of suspicion and distrust which have always been important factors in the attitudes between the two halves of the country. Southerners continued to look on the Northerners as being over-zealous to the point of diminishing returns, and slightly uncivilized in their readiness to do without the good things of life. Northerners looked on the Southerners as excessively individualistic and casual towards vital issues. Ho attempted to improve relations in early 1949 by sending Pham Van Dong and Pham Ngoc Thach to the South in order to show that the Viet Minh leaders in the North were keenly concerned with the state of affairs in the South and to appeal for closer adherence to the policy laid down by the Northern leadership. Despite Dong's efforts, things continued much the same as before, and it became apparent to Giap that in a military sense, the South could be only a side show. He had too weak a control system to be able to co-ordinate operations planned in the North and concerted into a national strategic pattern.

The major strategic implication of this separation between the North and the South was that the war had to be won in the North. If the French managed to annihilate or cripple Giap's main force, the entire movement would be set back many years, and so Giap had to act with caution. Had it been possible for Giap to have established his headquarters in Central Annam, the Viet Minh offensive might have been launched sooner than it was by a more daring assault on two fronts which would have tied the French reserves down and given the initiative to the Viet Minh. Instead, Giap had to reckon with the possibility of the French using all their mobile reserves, both land and air forces, against his opening offensive in Tonkin. At least Tonkin had two counterbalancing advantages for Giap: the French could not penetrate the Viet Bac with any ease, and to the north lay China which was then falling swiftly to the fast moving columns of the Red Army under Lin Piao.

Despite current notions that the Viet Minh had much less of a man power problem than the French, who for political reasons were unable to call on conscripts to maintain the strength of the Expeditionary Corps, the Viet Minh were able to field an army only three-quarters of the size of the French forces. Giap's army never exceeded 300,000, a fraction above one per cent of the population of Vietnam, while the French had 115,000 of their own men in Indo China, including the Foreign Legion and African colonial troops, and could also field nearly 300,000 Indo Chinese, most of whom were Vietnamese. The Viet Minh had two major problems in increasing the size of their forces. First it was difficult to recruit from the most heavily populated areas, because they were under French control; and second, the Viet Minh supply system could not cope with the needs of many more troops if they were fully employed on forward operations.

Ho attempted to minimize the recruiting problem by introducing on 4 November 1949, nation-wide conscription of all men and women above the age of eighteen. Implementation of this decree was not easy and it was not often resorted to, for the supply of volunteers was usually (although not always) equal to the high wastage rates caused by casualties and sickness. The Viet Minh leaders were, of course, fully conscious of the political advantages to be gained by adhering to the concept of a voluntary 'liberation army', and all soldiers were referred to in propaganda as if they were volunteers, irrespective of their method of recruitment.

The logistical problems of the Viet Minh continually confronted Giap, and he felt unable to undertake operations with a justifiable prospect of success until he knew that his lack of supplies was not going to reduce severely the strategic and tactical options available. The defensive actions of 1947 and 1948 did not call for huge amounts of supplies, and by dint of much sacrifice, the Viet Minh were able to survive in Bac Kan on local resources. However, this was no basis for the future, particularly since in 1948 the Thai government and the Chinese Nationalists had changed their policies of contributing to the support of the Viet Minh.

Local improvements were made through blocks of land (to be granted after the revolution had succeeded) being given as payment for arms, and through the establishment of secret workshops for arms manufacture. The simple weapons required for local guerrilla operations—mines, booby traps, grenades and small calibre bullets—could all be made in primitive but ingenious factories under the direction of engineer Tran Dai Nghia, who returned from France with Ho Chi Minh. When the Viet Minh had withdrawn from Hanoi they had been careful to take with them every item of machinery which they could move. Factories were built in the Viet Bac for the production of medium calibre weapons and ammunition and by 1949, one factory was producing 120 mm. mortars. The output of these factories is not known, but available information suggests that during 1948 the Viet Minh produced by themselves at least enough ammunition to permit the training of a few thousand men at any one time.

The real solution to Giap's logistical problems lay through the Chinese Communists. Close contact during the years after World War II enabled the Viet Minh High Command to form an accurate picture of events in China, and to estimate the amount of material support which the Chinese would give them as soon as Chiang Kai-shek was defeated. It seems highly likely that Giap knew that little assistance, other than training facilities for a few specialists, would be forthcoming until 1950. After 1950 he could expect to obtain most of his operational needs from his fellow Communists across the border. The fact that Giap commenced his major offensive in late

1950 indicates that the situation in China played a large if not dominant role in determining his own strategies for 1948 and 1949. Supplies were not his only problem, for he had to recruit and train his army. Once he had done this, he could not afford to indulge in wild assaults on the French, because his Viet Bac force was the *sine qua non* of the revolution. However, the two-year respite between Valluy's offensive and the availability of Chinese support was about as much time as he needed for forming and training his army, so that most factors pointed to remaining on the defensive until 1950.

It is interesting to speculate on the causes for the general Viet Minh acceptance of the doctrine of the protracted war. Did Giap really appreciate his long term political strength in contrast with that of the French, or were his conclusions drawn from much more obvious factors connected with events in China? If we exclude these more mundane factors as influences on Giap's thinking, then we ought to rate very highly his ability as a grand strategist. However, if we assume that he had some reliable inside knowledge of Mao's prospects, it becomes easier to explain his success without making extraordinary claims for his strategic abilities.

Chinese capacity to deliver supplies rose swiftly after 1950. In 1951, Giap obtained between ten and twenty tons per month from China. In 1952 this monthly flow had increased to 250 tons, in 1953 to 600 tons, in early 1954 to 1,500 tons, and after Dien Bien Phu it was running at 4,000 tons per month.[8] The transportation of these supplies was always difficult. The Chinese roads and railways could cope with the flow as far as the Tonkinese border, but from there it had to be carried largely by teams of coolies. The number of trucks available to the Viet Minh in 1950 was negligible, but Chinese donations provided over 1,000 heavy Molotovas during the succeeding four years. Giap planned the construction of several new roads across the Viet Bac, linking the Chinese supply heads of Ta Lung and P'ing-hsiang which lay close to Route 4 in the north-

[8]George K. Tanham. *Communist Revolutionary Warfare: the Viet Minh in Indo China* (Methuen, London, 1962), p. 69; *Communist Revolutionary Warfare: From the Viet Minh to the Viet Cong* (rev. ed., Frederick A. Praeger, New York, 1967).

east with the Red River valley and the routes which skirted around the Red River delta leading to the Viet Minh base areas in northern Annam. However, until he had annihilated the French chain of border posts, Giap was unable to use the main communication links with China, the roads and the Chinese railway, and traffic had to go by narrow tracks through the more deserted parts of the border mountains, much as it had done during World War II.

However, it was necessary to have the vast numbers of coolies to carry the supplies into Tonkin ready and organized before the Chinese Communists had reached the border. Experiments conducted in the Viet Bac showed that some 40,000 porters were needed to sustain an infantry division at a moderate operational pace. To supply an army of 300,000, a portering force of over 1,000,000 was needed. Unlike the regular soldiers, these people did not have to be recruited and moved from their home areas, for the coolies had to be scattered widely throughout the country. Some few hundred thousand were obtained from the local population of the Viet Bac and the surrounding provinces, and these provided the labour force for the headquarters and the regular troops when they were not engaged on forward operations. The remainder stayed in or near their native villages, supporting themselves as normal peasants when not on carrying missions. When they were required to carry supplies, efforts were made to see that they worked along the same general routes and over the same stages, so that they became expert at moving the greatest amounts as quickly as possible through their area of responsibility. Performance norms were worked out by Giap's supply staff so that accurate planning could be achieved. Some of these norms were:

> 55 lb. of rice or 33-44 lb. of arms over 15.5 miles of easy country by day or 12.4 miles by night.
> 28 lb. of rice or 22-33 lb. of arms over 9 miles of mountainous country by day or 7.5 miles by night.
> A buffalo cart could move 770 lb. over 7.5 miles per day.
> A horse cart could move 473 lb. over 12.4 miles per day.[9]

⁹Tanham, *op. cit.*, p. 70

With all these problems of general strategy on his mind, it is not surprising that Giap attempted very little in the way of offensive operations before 1950. In 1948 he concentrated on making the French position at Bac Kan as intolerable as possible so that they might come to regard it as more of a liability than an asset, and pull out. This would free Giap of a certain amount of concern lest it should be used as a bridge-head for some future French offensive. After the French withdrawal into Cao Bang in August 1948, Valluy began to plan a small offensive directed at Viet Minh supply centres in the Red River valley within fifty miles of Hanoi, particularly Viet Tri and Son Tay. These thrusts were made in November 1948, and yielded large quantities of Communist supplies. However, Giap was well aware of the risks attendant on hold-ing supplies so close to the French main position, and the amounts lost were far from crucial.

During 1949, Giap began to increase the pressure on Route 4 and on Lao Kay, forcing the French garrisons of the many border posts to stay within their defences much more than they had been doing. The long stretches of country between these posts were then opened up for unrestricted Viet Minh move-ment. Clearly Giap's immediate aim was to wipe out the French presence along the central and eastern parts of the Sino-Tonkinese border. Was this the best plan in the circum-stances? Certainly it suffered from the disadvantage of pre-dictability. The French had been given sufficient time to fortify their posts strongly, and it would cost a great number of casualties to take them. Had Giap moved against some of the more isolated French posts in central and western Tonkin, he could have achieved surprise and opened up a good com-munications link for advances into Laos and to the south of the Red River delta. However, to leave the French border forts intact in his rear would have been to expose himself to interdiction of his supply routes, and his headquarters would have been an attractive and vulnerable target to the French, once they knew that Giap's main force was no longer protect-ing the Viet Bac. Hence, although he could not hope to achieve strategic surprise, as distinct from tactical surprise, Giap would have been most unwise to have launched an offensive without first securing his rear and his supply lines from China.

The French, presumably in ignorance of Giap's strength and capability, decided to hold the main towns along Route 4 between Lang Son and Cao Bang and to withdraw several of the smaller intermediate posts. They abandoned some of the less defensible posts in the wild, roadless country between Cao Bang and Ha Giang, but left a sprinkling of garrisons dotted about covering the approaches to the Red River valley from the north. None of these posts were as strong as those along Route 4, and so a series of attacks against them could serve as a rehearsal for the major assault on the Cao Bang-Lang Son line. The distance between Cao Bang and Lao Kay, some 150 miles, made a co-ordinated simultaneous attack on both fronts impracticable, and so Giap naturally chose the easier target. The first sizeable attacks against the Lao Kay area were made in 1949, during the change from the dry season to the wet in April and June. Giap had allowed his battalions to make the long journey during the dry months, and had chosen for the time of attack the period when French pursuit would be most hampered. These attacks did not have sufficient force to eject the French from their outposts around Lao Kay—perhaps the attacks were not meant to achieve this—and the Viet Minh melted away again. However, the weight of their supporting fire made clear to the French officers that their military superiority was dwindling fast.

In late 1949 and early 1950, after the Chinese Communists had established control over Yunnan and Kwangsi, facilities for the amalgamation of Giap's regiments into divisions became available. Working on a pattern of four regiments to a division, Giap was able to form four infantry divisions of over 12,000 men each in the Viet Bac and one in Northern Annam. The divisions in the Viet Bac were numbered 304, 308, 312 and 316, while the one in Northern Annam was known as 320 Division. The Chinese provided large amounts of artillery and established two practice ranges for the Viet Minh at Tsingsi and at Longchow. Officers were sent to special staff courses in Southern China, and Chinese advisers and technicians came into the Viet Bac. The regiments came together and exercised as divisions around the Chinese practice ranges. The regimental commanders became highly skilled in the use of the new artillery support, which gave them the strength to overcome a French battalion position. The divisional commanders learned to manoeuvre their regiments over wide areas so that they could ambush and trap large French columns moving along the roads which linked the main garrison positions.

The last weeks of the dry season of early 1950 saw a renewal of the attacks around Lao Kay. This time, the Viet Minh were able to strike far harder than in the previous year. Posts such as Pho Lu on the Red River, Nha Do in the mountains twenty miles north of the river, and several in the mountains around Pa Kha were either overrun by 308 Division or menaced so directly that they were abandoned. Lao Kay and several of the other posts nearby remained in French hands but the reason

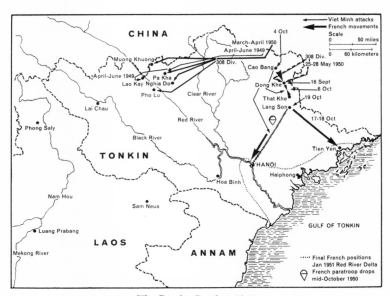

The Border Battles, 1950

for this was less French determination than Giap's reluctance
to risk taking on too much. Lao Kay survived for another wet
season but nobody there felt at all optimistic on looking forward to the next dry season.

308 Division broke off the attacks around Lao Kay in April
1950 and returned to the country between Cao Bang and
Lang Son. Although Giap had been developing his plan for
finally ejecting the French from the eastern border region
he was not yet ready. Perhaps he wanted more proof that his
units were capable of achieving what he was about to set them.
Not only did these units need final polishing in attacking
French positions held by several hundred men, but Giap
needed to know what capacity the French had to reinforce or
counter-attack. From what we now know of the happenings
along the Chinese border in 1950, it seems that Giap had
formulated his basic strategy for ousting the French in the
early months of the year. The main French garrisons were at
Cao Bang and Lang Son. Route 4 was held between Lang
Son and That Khe, where a battalion was stationed. Beyond
That Khe the road was abandoned to the Viet Minh save for
the intermediate staging post of Dong Khe, which was also
held by a battalion. Dong Khe is fourteen miles by road from
That Khe and twenty four from Cao Bang. The garrison at
Cao Bang had only three means of withdrawal: southward
through the Viet Bac along Route 3; by airlift direct to Lang
Son; and by Route 4 to Lang Son. From what Giap knew of
the French, the third method seemed the most likely to be
adopted—the first was too foolhardy and the second too
ignominious—and so he concentrated on taking complete
control of Route 4 between That Khe and Cao Bang. The best
way of achieving this was to take out the garrison at Dong
Khe.

This battalion fortress was not only typical of all French
fortresses in Tonkin, but it was the smallest along the road,
and seemed a good point for testing French contingency
reactions when the security of the post was severely threatened.
Therefore 308 Division was launched into an attack against

Dong Khe as soon as it had recovered from its long walk back from Lao Kay. The wet season had begun and mists shrouded the mountains which ringed the Dong Khe hollow, effectively removing the French air force as a factor in the battle. The whole division encircled the fortifications at some distance and started a two day artillery bombardment on 25 May. Only after the main defences had been shattered by the weight of the fire did the four battalions designated for the final assault storm the fortress in the early hours of 28 May. Later that morning the mist cleared and the French counter-attacked with a paratroop battalion. Apparently the Viet Minh were unprepared for this move and they were swept out of the town and kept out until a ground relief column from That Khe made its way through. 308 Division then disappeared to report their lessons to Giap and to make better preparations for their next test.

Giap now had the information he needed to finalize his plans. He chose September to launch his offensive, capitalizing on the prevalent ground mists of the late wet season, and on the early months of the dry season, to simplify the consolidation of his gains and his advance through the mountains to confront the French in their ultimate stronghold, the Red River delta. His plan was to surround Cao Bang and That Khe, creating apprehension in the minds of the French commanders; to take Dong Khe, thereby closing the land link between the two besieged garrisons; and to wait for either or both to attempt to get through to one another. Once forced out of their fortifications into the open country, the moving French soldiers would be extremely vulnerable to ambushes and Giap hoped that he would be able to wipe out these garrisons without the costly losses which assaulting them would entail.

There is no doubt that this plan was a good one. The French had placed themselves in a very weak position through trying to hold a single line with nothing behind it, so that they could only move forces along this line in response to any Viet Minh pressure. To prevent the French from moving their forces, all Giap had to do was to make a small cut in the line, while to

destroy the French he could devour the isolated sections of
line piecemeal. The French might have given Giap some concern by refusing to budge from behind their defences and by
depending entirely on air re-supply. However, even these
modern means could not have saved the French, for Giap had
enough artillery, and the terrain gave him enough vantage
points for deploying it decisively, to restrict the air traffic to
such an extent that the French could not have sat within their
fortifications indefinitely. Because the French High Command,
in ignorance of the true strength of the Viet Minh and keenly
conscious of the dishonour of retreating before lesser breeds,
had chosen a plan involving its troops in a high degree of risk,
Giap was able to launch his offensive with a very low degree
of risk. He was one of those few generals fortunate enough to
be able to make a reputation before running the risk of losing
it.

The offensive went according to plan. On 16 September
1950 the Viet Minh took Dong Khe for the second time. The
French did not dare to drop in another battalion of paratroops
to try to regain it. Instead they launched an overland thrust
from That Khe and ordered the evacuation of Cao Bang.
General Carpentier, the French Commander in Chief, hoped
that the force from That Khe would brush the Viet Minh aside
and retake Dong Khe before moving on up Route 4 to link
up with the smaller force from Cao Bang and escort it to safety.
The force from That Khe was ambushed before it had reached
Dong Khe and the Cao Bang garrison had to hasten to the
assistance of its would-be rescuer, falling into the same ambush
from the opposite direction. Five thousand French soldiers
were killed or captured, all their equipment went to assist
Giap's quartermasters, and only a handful of desperately weary
men struggled back to That Khe.

Those who reached That Khe after 10 October were too late
because the swift advance of the Viet Minh had made its tenure
extremely dangerous and exposed its garrison to the same fate
as befell the men from Cao Bang. By 12 October, effective
French resistance north of Lang Son had ceased, and the eighty

miles of Route 4 between Cao Bang and Lang Son had fallen to Giap. The next obstacle to be cleared was Lang Son. The French knew that Giap was closing on their main base in the north-east with up to three divisions, and that their only hope was withdrawal. Two battalions of paratroops were unable to open Route 1 to Hanoi, and panic reigned at Lang Son. The only hope was to flee down Route 4 to the coast at Mon Kay before Giap's divisions had cut that leg also. On the night between 17 and 18 October, the base was evacuated in great haste, leaving intact for the Viet Minh huge stocks of supplies including 13 field guns, 125 mortars, 450 trucks, three platoons of tanks, 940 machine guns, 1,200 sub-machine guns, more than 8,000 rifles and 1,100 tons of ammunition. Even worse, the French had lost over 6,000 troops, killed and captured, while Viet Minh casualties had been light. The balance of forces for the struggle which was to take place around the Red River delta had tipped a long way against the French.

In November 1950, Carpentier decided that further evacuations were necessary. Thai Nguyen, captured only ten days previously, was abandoned. Hoa Binh, the Muong capital on the Black River and sally port for the French to raid the Viet Minh supply route which linked the Viet Bac with the Communist-dominated Northern Annam, also had to be relinquished. The most severe loss was Lao Kay. The last remaining French point on the Chinese border, protector of the natural communications axis from China, the Red River, was in danger of becoming cut off by Viet Minh columns which had made the thousand yard crossing of the flooded Red River and were marching to close the tracks to Lai Chau, sixty miles to the south-west. The garrison of Lao Kay withdrew with the Viet Minh less than half an hour behind it. After struggling through a series of ambushes and rear guard actions it reached safety when the Viet Minh ran out of supplies.

By the end of 1950, the whole of the Chinese border was under Viet Minh control, and Giap was free to move his divisions anywhere he liked north of the Red River between China and the delta. His refuge and base, the Viet Bac, had survived the years of weakness, and the tactical initiative lay in his hands. The French now began to entertain fears for their position in the Red River delta, and plans were made for the evacuation of women and children. Carpentier even envisaged the entire surrender of Tonkin in 1951. Giap had developed his doctrines, raised and trained his army, and successfully fought his first major campaign. However, he had enjoyed many advantages, not least of which was French ignorance of his strength, which led them to make the initial going very easy for him. While the campaigns of 1950 showed that Giap had an excellent grasp of the details of building an army, they did not test him to the point at which his reputation as a great commander and strategist can be said to have been established. Perhaps in view of what was to happen in 1951, even Giap himself would not wish to be regarded as having reached his strategic apogee by 1950.

5 The Misdirected Offensive

Before we can criticize Giap's use of the initiative he had won so clearly in the border battles of late 1950, it is necessary to look at both the overall aim of the Viet Minh and the way in which Giap's strategy in 1951 served that aim. The re-establishment of Ho Chi Minh's authority required that the greater part of the Vietnamese population be brought under Viet Minh rule. Despite the large proportion of the countryside under the control of Giap's men, the two main population centres, the Red River delta and southern Cochin China from Saigon to the Bassac River, remained in the hands of the French. Therefore the Viet Minh had to break the French hold over one at least of these areas before it was demonstrably able to govern a large part of the Vietnamese population. This much is easy to formulate but severe complications arise when one considers whether this obviously political aim could be achieved entirely by military means, or by a combination of military and political offensives.

While there is much to be said for applying a predominantly political solution to a political problem, Ho's position in early 1951 was totally different to any he had yet held. Now he had the military strength to make the French feel insecure in a military sense, and this was evidenced by their orders to evacuate all French women and children from the Red River delta area by early 1951. If he could somehow make the

French pull their troops out of one of the main areas of population concentration, he would be able to take a short cut to
political control by then applying his cadres to this population
group without any risk of French interference.

The attractiveness of this plan is obvious, but two difficulties stood in its way. First, Ho and Giap had to decide whether
it was feasible to make the French relinquish one of these
areas and second, which area should be selected as the target.
The apparent ease of answering the second question possibly
had a great deal to do with the answer given to the first,
instead of the factors which had a more direct bearing on an
objective answer being permitted to be the decisive influences.
The most fundamental fact was that French defensive strength
both in the Red River delta and around Saigon was formidable. French numbers and air power gave them the capacity
to concentrate greater numbers of troops for the defence than
the Viet Minh could for the attack. Certainly, as the border
battles had shown, numbers were not everything in this war,
but the whole nature of the areas to be defended gave the
French much more chance to use their mechanical mobility,
their firepower and their monopoly of the air to devastating
effect than did the mist shrouded, jungle-clad mountains of the
border region.

Taking the war to the main French bridgeheads greatly
shortened the French lines of supply and lengthened those of
the Viet Minh. Although the Chinese had begun to supply
appreciable amounts of aid, it was by no means sufficient to
offset the greater availability of materials, the fewer risks in
transit and the shorter time lags enjoyed by the French. Giap's
only means of moving large amounts of supplies was by
coolies and ox-carts, and his ammunition and food crawled
across the countryside at three miles an hour and arrived
piece by piece, mostly in thirty-three pound lots. Skilful planning and a careful build-up beforehand could make this
system adequate for fighting a large battle at any one particular point, but it was too inflexible to permit a sudden shift
of the point of thrust over any appreciable distance. Thus,

once Giap had begun an attack in one locality, he was unable to exploit French weakness arising elsewhere as more French reserves became committed to the battle. The French, however, through their use of vehicles and their advantage of operating on interior lines, had the capacity for rapid re-disposition of their forces, and so could afford to over-concentrate at the point of attack, and leave weak forces elsewhere, to be reinforced with safety at the first signs that Giap was preparing to alter his plan.

In view of these advantages which the French enjoyed, it would seem that on the evidence available to Giap in late 1950, his chances of forcing the French out of one of their two main base areas were slim, and hence the Viet Minh would be much better advised to avoid a frontal confrontation in an effort to oust the French. However, Giap was not making these decisions in an ivory tower, comfortably isolated from environmental pressures. The war against the French had been in progress for four years, and during this time much hardship and frustration had been inflicted on Ho and his supporters. The possibility of ending the difficulties which accompanied life in the remote jungles of Tonkin must have seemed very tempting. Furthermore, Ho could not afford to take for granted the support of the peasants in the French-controlled areas: there were sufficient remnants of the anti-Communist political parties to form nuclei capable of expansion if serious popular disillusionment with Viet Minh failure to make visible progress against the French became prevalent. Therefore there were powerful reasons which justified the Viet Minh High Command in taking some risks in order to consolidate their political position. It must be noted, however, that neither of these reasons actually required the Viet Minh to take control of the Red River delta or the Saigon area. All that they demanded was some progress in this direction.

While it is not possible to state the amount of influence which these arguments carried within the Viet Minh leadership, we know from what followed their deliberation that they chose to attempt to crush the French Army in the Red River delta by a frontal offensive. This decision was made fairly plain to all in the delta by the Viet Minh propaganda announcements of January 1951 that Ho Chi Minh would be in Hanoi for *Tet*, i.e. in February. Unfortunately for Giap, someone else had come to Hanoi in January; General Jean de Lattre de Tassigny, France's most outstanding senior commander, had been sent to take both political and military command in Indo China and restore the situation after the debâcle of late 1950. De Lattre perceived the strategic importance of the Red River delta and, after a tour of inspection, set thousands of men to work preparing to resist a Viet Minh assault. He forbade the evacuation of the women and children and, through his driving although enigmatic personality, rebuilt the confidence of the French soldiers in their ability to conduct a successful defensive battle.

Giap, in making his aim a direct attack on the French in the delta, was contradicting a number of principles laid down by one of the few really great strategic thinkers, Sun Tzu, who wrote in China during the fourth century B.C. and who laid the foundations for much of Mao Tse-tung's military thought. Sun Tzu has summed up some of his thoughts thus:

> Supreme excellence consists in breaking the enemy's resistance without fighting.
> Thus the highest form of generalship is to baulk the enemy's plans; the next best is to prevent the junction of the enemy's forces; the next in order is to attack the enemy's army in the field; the worst policy of all is to besiege walled cities.

and

> To refrain from intercepting an enemy whose banners are in perfect order, to refrain from attacking an army drawn up in calm and confident array—this is the art of studying circumstances.

By displaying so much contempt for the principles of Sun Tzu, Giap revealed a similar attitude towards Mao Tse-tung. It would be ridiculous to ascribe this to anything other than

General Vo Nguyen Giap

Giap (standing) discusses plans before the battle of Dien Bien Phu at a meeting of the Political Bureau of the Party Central Committee. Ho Chi Minh is second from left

Viet Minh transport on the road to Dien Bien Phu
—*Vietnam Peoples Army*

A Viet Minh bamboo bridge
—*Vietnam Peoples Army*

General Giap, Commander-in-Chief of the Viet Minh forces, giving orders
to his divisional commanders and staff officers
—*Vietnam Peoples Army*

Giap inspects anti-aircraft artillery
—*Vietnam Peoples Army*

insufficient thought about wider matters of strategy, a common enough fault amongst senior military commanders, but one which might have been avoided had Giap received some formal tuition in the history of strategic thought before he rose to the height of Viet Minh Commander in Chief.

One significant factor of which Giap seems to have made no use was the French propensity for the attack. Ever since de Lattre's earliest days in the French Army, the prevalent tactical doctrines had been *élan* (dash) and *offensive à outrance* (offensive without limit). While strategic notions had taken refuge in the defensive posture of the Maginot Line, the doctrine of the offensive had remained of sufficient tactical importance to be restored to the level of strategy in the last year of World War II, in de Lattre's handling of the First French Army. The events of late 1951, when de Lattre seized Hoa Binh, have shown that the change of wars and environment had by no means removed his desire to be on the offensive and to keep the initiative, and so Giap would have been justified in planning on the basis that the French would begin to think offensively as soon as they felt that the immediate threat to the security of the Red River delta had receded.

The deduction to be drawn from this factor had been spelled out for Giap by Sun Tzu:

All warfare is based on deception. Hence, when able to attack, we must seem unable; when using our forces, we must seem inactive; when we are near we must make the enemy believe that we are far away; when far away, we must make him believe we are near. Hold out baits to entice the enemy. Feign disorder, and crush him.

While it would not be fair to blame a man with the informal training of Giap for not knowing the writings of the elder Moltke, they are too apposite to be omitted from this discussion:

A clever military leader will succeed in many cases in choosing defensive positions of such an offensive nature from the strategic point of view that the enemy is compelled to attack us in them.

In other words, Giap would surely have achieved far more than his frontal attacks on the Red River delta in 1951 could do, by attempting to lure the French out from behind their defences on to his own ground. There by fighting on ground of his own choosing, Giap could have offset most of the advantages held by the French in the delta and probably inflicted such a defeat on the French that the subsequent collapse of morale, all the greater since de Lattre was involved, would have brought a Viet Minh victory much nearer than it was in mid-1951.

It is remarkable that Giap showed no sign of having grasped this strategic principle until late 1953, despite the obvious demonstrations of its power implicit in his defeats of French offensives made into his own area in late 1951 at Hoa Binh and late 1952 at Phu Doan and the Chan Muong Gorge. There were many variations of this principle which Giap could have put into effect to weaken the Red River delta position. He could have lured the French out to one great battle or to a number, in a way similar to Slim's strategy at Imphal and Kohima. Once the French had become locked in battle with Giap's main force, he could have called out the guerrillas and regional forces to rise up in the rear of the French, cutting them off from supplies by ambushing the roads, blowing up the bridges and congesting the roads with civilians. The French Army, partially strangled, could then have been worn away gradually as at Dien Bien Phu—but three years earlier.

In criticizing the Viet Minh for their crude notions of strategy in 1951, it is difficult to know exactly where to place the blame, for not only were decisions like this made collectively but they were also influenced by a Chinese advisory group which Mao Tse-tung had sent to Ho Chi Minh. The leader of this group, General Lo K'uei-po, was a man of much military experience, although his experience was of a different war to that which the Viet Minh were fighting. It is possible that at the outset his opinions carried much sway with Giap. However, Lo K'uei-po's function was as an advisor, not as a commander, despite Hoang Van Chi's allegations to the contrary, and it seems extremely unlikely that, had Giap conceived a more subtle strategy for overcoming the Red River delta, he would have put aside his better judgment and allowed the inferior ideas of a foreigner to carry away the lives of many thousands of Vietnamese troops for little gain, particularly in view of the Viet Minh object—national independence.

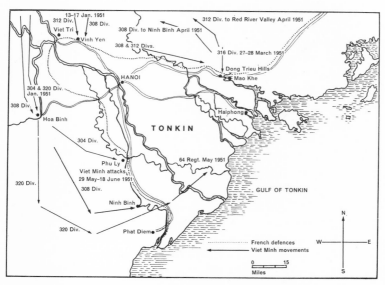

The Battles for the Red River Delta, 1951

The point which Giap selected to penetrate the Red River delta was the small town of Vinh Yen, thirty miles to the north-west of Hanoi. The mountains of the Viet Bac thrust out a long spine, the Tam Dao Massif, to within ten miles of Vinh Yen and twenty of Hanoi. This ridge was jungle-covered, and deeply dissected by steep valleys; it ascended to a height of over 4,000 feet and was easily the best covered approach for a force attempting to seize Hanoi. Two main roads led south-

wards into Vinh Yen from the mountains and Route 2 linked
the town with Hanoi, an hour's drive or two days' walk away.
The plain around Vinh Yen was very flat with poor drainage
to the Red River, ten miles to the south. Consequently much
of it was paddy field, suitable in the wet season only for
infantry, but offering no obstacle to mechanized vehicles in
the dry season which, in January, was some three months old.
Immediately to the south of Vinh Yen was a shallow lake, the
Dam Vac, some three miles from east to west and several
hundred yards across, which formed an excellent obstacle to
French movement. In effect, the French were fighting with
their backs to a wall. On the northern side of Vinh Yen was
an arc of low hills rising to a few hundred feet above the plain,
their crest line some three miles from the town and their slopes
covered in thick scrub.

The topography of the area made Vinh Yen an admirable
point for Giap to attack and advance through to sieze Hanoi
quickly. By the same token, these characteristics made the
French realize the potential of Vinh Yen for Giap's purpose
and they were on their guard against any attack. Thus Giap
had lost strategic surprise by selecting Vinh Yen, and he had
to rely on tactical surprise for a cheap victory. The size of the
force he had allocated to the assault, the 20,000 men of 308
and 312 Divisions, made complete concealment of his intentions difficult and French intelligence was aware of the Viet
Minh build-up in the Tam Dao mountains. Two mobile groups
had been stationed to defend the approaches to Vinh Yen,
each consisting of three battalions of infantry and a battalion
of artillery, and supported by tanks and engineers totalling
over three thousand men per group.

Giap's tactical plan was to divide these two mobile groups,
ambush one and then crush the other. The ambush was baited
by a diversionary attack on the small French outpost of Bao
Chuc several miles north-west of Vinh Yen. One of the French
groups rashly raced to the assistance of the fifty defenders of
Bao Chuc and fell into the ambush which had been laid near
Dao Tu. Although the French lost the best part of a battalion

in the ambush it was not as successful as Giap had hoped; most of the group was able to withdraw into Vinh Yen under the cover of an intensive artillery and air barrage. However, the Viet Minh were left in command of the northern hills and a three mile gap in the French defences had been opened up to the east of Vinh Yen. By the evening of the first day of the assault, 13 January 1951, the French had been forced back to the Dam Vac.

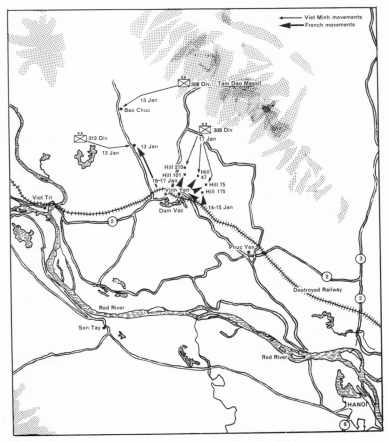

The Battle of Vinh Yen, 13-17 January 1951

De Lattre appreciated that the fighting around Vinh Yen was the awaited offensive for Hanoi and on the following day flew in to Vinh Yen and took personal charge of the battle. He ordered an airlift of reserves to be flown up from Saigon and placed all available aircraft in Tonkin on stand-by for bombarding Giap's attack waves. A third mobile group was brought to the battlefield from the east and the Viet Minh were cleared off the low hills to the north and east of the town. Why Giap did not take this opportunity to cripple de Lattre by conducting a defensive battle from the relative security of the high ground is something of a mystery. Perhaps he felt that he had lured the French out into a weaker defensive position where they could be overrun more easily than close to Vinh Yen.

He gave the French two hours of consolidation on the hill crest and then launched his attack with the whole of 308 Division at 5 p.m. on 17 January. This blow was successful in the central sector but the Viet Minh were unable to dislodge the French from two hilltops on either flank. The defensive battle which developed around them turned out to the French advantage through de Lattre's use of air attacks on to the massing Viet Minh. Giap called the attack off at noon on 18 January and the Viet Minh departed into the Tam Dao mountains leaving 6,000 dead and 500 prisoners in French hands. Probably another 8,000 had been wounded, and so Vinh Yen had cost Giap the fighting strength of two divisions until the remnants could be re-formed into their original units and reinforcements supplied.

After the battle, Giap was in a very bad position, but was wise enough to conduct a full investigation into the reasons for his defeat. He passed some of the blame on to his troops, accusing them of lack of aggressiveness, and even of cowardice. However, this had been the first major reverse for the Viet Minh in four years of fighting, and spirits were sufficiently high for the setback to be absorbed without serious splits appearing within the leadership. Giap could rationalize that every general ought to be allowed one mistake. He felt that his fundamental idea, the need for a direct attack on the French in the Red River delta, was still correct. Next time, however, he would not pick such an obvious target for his assault.

Several high-level conferences of Communist leaders were held in the Viet Bac after the battle. The Viet Minh troops must have been a little disillusioned with the promises of this leadership when yet another *Tet* had to be spent deep in the Tonkinese jungles. They soon had other things to think about for in early March Ho announced the formation of a supposedly new political organization to lead the struggle against the French, the *Lao Dong* or Workers' Party. This party was a natural successor to the Communist Party which Ho had pretended to disband in late 1945 in order to rally non-Communist support behind his government. Ho must have felt the need for a new stiffener for his followers, for in permitting the emergence of a strong Communist movement the last vestiges of the facade that his movement was primarily nationalist were thrown away, and the world could see that if he achieved power, Vietnam would certainly become yet another People's Democracy.

By this stage, Giap had begun to plan his second attempt to break through the French defences and had shifted his attention to the second most important point for the French, the port of Haiphong, through which came most of their supplies and reinforcements. The French perimeter was only twenty miles to the north of Haiphong and a convenient range of hills, the Dong Trieu Massif, approached to within a very short distance of the French defences. Also of strategic importance were the coal mines which were situated in the north-eastern sector of the Red River delta in a seventy mile strip from Mao Khe in the west to Ke Bau Island in the east. An attack at Mao Khe offered Giap an appreciable degree of tactical surprise because of its distance from both Hanoi and Vinh Yen. There was sufficient rough country between the Viet Bac and the approaches to Mao Khe to permit large scale troop movements and concentration without a great degree of risk of discovery by the French and the lines of communication were adequate for the passage of large amounts of supplies.

The eastern side of the delta was a dangerous area in which to launch an assault on the French because of French naval power. The French perimeter ran within a few miles of either the sea or deep channels for sixty miles along the northern edge of the delta and for another sixty miles hugging the coast up to Mon Cay on the Chinese border. Destroyers could patrol within a few miles of this front and could support the defenders at any threatened point with far more firepower than was usually available from land bound artillery. Assault craft could thicken up this fire support and could rapidly transport reinforcements to strengthen those parts of the line which came under heavy pressure. It seems doubtful that Giap really appreciated the strength of the French in this region.

Given the assumption that an attack had to be made in the north-east of the delta, there were several good reasons for choosing Mao Khe as the point to breach. It was a small post between the strong points of Dong Trieu and Uong Bi, it was as far from the open sea as possible while still having a direct access route to Haiphong, and it was in the shadow of the Dong Son hills which offered a good forming-up area from which the attack could be launched. If Giap had gone further to the east, much larger naval forces could have been brought to bear on him than at Mao Khe, and his routes to Haiphong would have been cut by several estuaries, forcing him to take a long and devious advance and giving the French sufficient time to organize a counter-attack. Had he attacked much to the west of Mao Khe he would have faced much stronger defences; the hills were much further away and the open terrain gave the defenders a considerable advantage over the attackers. Whatever may be said of Giap's strategy in moving his weight against the eastern region of the delta, his selection of the precise point for the attack is very difficult to criticize.

The force chosen to make the break-through was the unblooded 316 Division which was moved into the Dong Trieu hills in mid-March. 304 and 320 Divisions were given the role of making diversionary attacks on the western edge of the French defences on the Day River, to draw off the French

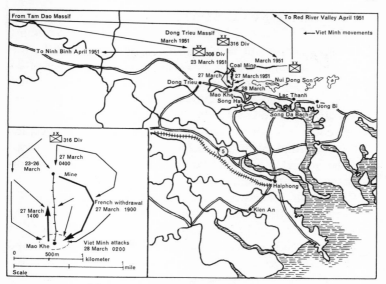

The Battle of Mao Khe, 23-28 March 1951

reserves. 308 and 312 Divisions moved into the Dong Trieu hills to act as general support for 316 Division. Perhaps they had also been given the task of exploiting the break-through once it had been made, flooding the delta with over 30,000 Viet Minh regulars. Facing the attackers were a chain of platoon posts several miles apart in the foothills, a company post at the Mao Khe mine, one mile north of the Mao Khe village, and another company supported by an armoured car platoon at Mao Khe itself.

The attack began on 23 March 1951 when the forward posts in the hills were overrun. De Lattre was presented with the problem of deciding whether this was Giap's main thrust or whether it was merely a feint. He responded cautiously with a minimal reinforcement of a paratroop battalion, three destroyers and two landing craft to halt the initial onslaught. The ensuing naval gunfire and aerial bombardment prevented the Viet Minh from getting into the Mao Khe post and forced Giap to halt in order to consolidate and re-group for a second

attack which began on 27 March and continued until the early
morning of 28 March. 316 Division succeeded in overrunning
the mine defences but the company had made a skilful withdrawal to the main village position during the evening of 27
March. The defenders of the village position put up such a
spirited battle that they were able to hold off the attacking
waves until the following day when once again French air
power could have been used with telling effect. Giap decided
at this stage that the attack had failed and withdrew his troops
into the Viet Bac to commence a new round of reconsideration, analysis and planning.

Viet Minh casualties amounted to over 2,000 and 400
bodies were left behind on the battlefield by the retreating
divisions. Once again, the Central Committee of the Lao
Dong had a difficult task to justify its conduct of the war and
the retention of Giap as commander, but the tightness of the
system of control was sufficient for Ho's needs. One wonders
how far his own trust in Giap's abilities was being stretched
during this period. Again we are faced with the peculiarly
strong political position which Giap enjoyed, having been one
of Ho's senior lieutenants for twelve years and having established a reputation of great competence as acting head of state
during 1946. While the question of Giap's dismissal for his
second failure arises inescapably in a Western context, it
would be far from the realities of Viet Minh politics to assume
that the same problems would even be seriously considered.
The closest approximation to Giap's position which Western
politics could offer would be an imaginary leader holding the
offices of both Defense Secretary McNamara and General
Westmoreland in 1968, who had occupied those positions
since 1956, played a leading role in restoring American government after the expulsion of a foreign occupying power in
1962, organized for the Democratic Party the suppression of
all Republicans, and in 1963 occupied the Presidency while
President Kennedy spent four months negotiating in Moscow.
The dismissal of such a man would be seen by the general
public as a grave attack on the entire revolutionary movement.

The main problem facing the Viet Minh leaders in April 1951 was whether to continue their attempts to break into the delta or to change the basic strategy to something less direct in approach. The fact that a third attempt was made indicates that Giap felt that each of the previous failures had been due to special circumstances which were not likely to be present at other points. At Vinh Yen he could point to the devastating effect of the French air attacks on his troops fighting across fairly open country. At Mao Khe, he could claim that the French navy had denied him the success which 316 Division came close to achieving. Therefore, if he could find another point to assault which gave protection from air attacks and which was not accessible to the navy, he ought to be successful.

While this reasoning is hypothetical, the topography of the third area which Giap selected for attack did go some way towards offsetting the French naval and air supremacy. The south-western sector of the French delta defences ran along the line of the Day River, a delta drainage channel which permitted the passage of very shallow draft vessels only. To the east of the Day River spread the flat expanses of paddy field mirroring the grey skies which dominated the delta during the floods of the wet season. The ground on the western side was of a totally different character, particularly between Phat Diem near the mouth of the river and Phu Ly, a large town nearly forty miles to the north. Not only was the west bank higher than the east, dominating vast stretches of the monotonous tiny rectangles of paddy field, but it was Karst country.

Tonkin has some of the largest areas of Karst in the world. Sheets of it, often over twenty miles across, are scattered liberally through the highlands, chiefly in the Viet Bac, but also occuring south of the Black River and on the western edge of the Red River delta. These tracts of compact or crystalline limestone form huge areas of stone abounding with pits of all sizes and interlaced by elongated hollows and ridges covered by low bush. No surface drainage is apparent, for rain water seeps through the limestone, dissolving the more soluble

rocks and leaving caverns of the cohesive limestone. Solution
sometimes also produces a complex fretting or fluting of the
surface so that extremely sharp edges point upward to cut the
feet or footwear of anyone rash enough to attempt to walk
across it for a long distance. However, this disadvantage was
of small significance to Giap compared with the protection
from air attack afforded by the pits and caves which broke up
the limestone at very frequent intervals. Not only could men
find refuge in the Karst country, but supply dumps could be
made almost invulnerable through location in caves or dispersal over a large number of shallow surface pits.

The Karst hills came to within two miles of Phu Ly, ran
directly alongside the Day River for fifteen miles, breaking
away from the river a few miles north of Ninh Binh and extending due south for another fifteen miles to flank the paddy
fields of Phat Diem. From where the Karst area separated
from the river, land communications were greatly complicated
by the maze of narrow waterways which flowed across the
paddy fields within fifteen miles of the coast at much more
frequent intervals than through the inland fields. Thus the
southern fifty miles of the Day River offered important advantages to Viet Minh attackers, while the problems of the
defence were greatly complicated by the difficulty of moving
reserves swiftly from one part of the sector to another.

Giap also decided to make much greater use of the Viet
Minh supporters who lived within the French dominated area.
Instead of leaving the entire task to the main force divisions
attacking from outside the delta, he spent several weeks in
building up a force which could suddenly rise up in the French
rear and prevent the dispatch of the mobile groups from place
to place. Enough Viet Minh soldiers had been recruited from
the delta inhabitants to form one main force regiment, the
42nd Independent Infantry, and another regiment was infiltrated secretly into the southern sector near Phat Diem. This
regiment, the 64th of 320 Division, concentrated near Thai
Binh, some thirty miles behind the French perimeter defences
and linked up with the 42nd Regiment. However, it is difficult

to perceive what effect Giap imagined would be achieved by two lightly armed regiments against several well equipped French mobile groups operating within a short distance of their main base. In the event, these infiltrated troops were unable to prevent the French from moving their reserves to the most threatened points and their contribution to Giap's main effort was very small. The most that can be said for this idea is that it showed an awareness on Giap's part that his strength was not confined to the offensive power of his main force divisions and that civilians behind the battle zones might be able to tie the French down sufficiently to tilt the balance of military power.

During the last weeks of the dry season, Giap moved his forces into place for the opening of the battle of the Day River. His initial objective was the Catholic controlled area of the bishoprics of Phat Diem and Bui Chu. If the Viet Minh could control this area, the morale of the anti-Communist Vietnamese in the delta would be seriously affected. The main thrust was to be made by 320 Division on the right flank, working into Phat Diem. 304 Division was to draw off French reserves to the north by attacking Phu Ly and 308 Division was to pin down the French in the central sector by an assault on Ninh Binh. While these divisions were moving into their concentration areas, French attention was distracted by 312 Division which made several small probes on the north-western corner of the delta and then moved west towards the Red River valley near Yen Bay, from which they could threaten the first French outpost in the T'ai hills, Nghia Lo. The French were not deceived by these moves and remained within their defences while 312 Division made some preliminary reconnaissances of the south bank of the Red River in preparation for the next dry season's campaign.

The wet season broke in early May, complicating Giap's supply problems, but giving additional protection from air attack through poor visibility. By late May all was ready, and Giap launched the northern and central assaults on the 29th, followed up, once these battles had developed, by the southern

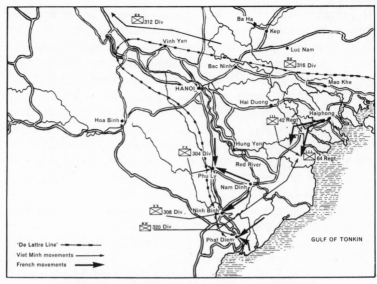

The Battles of the Day River, 29 May—18 June 1951

thrust against Phat Diem. The French immediately moved in over one division of reinforcements and sent patrols of naval landing craft carrying troops and artillery up the Day River. The Viet Minh were successful in gaining several bridgeheads on the east bank but the skill of the naval patrols and the determination of the French defenders, particularly at Ninh Binh where de Lattre's only son was killed, prevented them from making appreciable advances. The naval actions on the Day River were crucial in cutting the Viet Minh supply links, and Giap's offensive began to bog down. Another impediment was the lack of co-operation shown to the Viet Minh by many of the delta peasants. The Catholic areas had organized their own militia to resist the Viet Minh and these units fought stubbornly, holding up the Viet Minh until the French saw that the main thrust was coming from the south and sent reinforcements.

The battle wore on until mid-June. Giap made no further gains, his casualties grew alarmingly, and his supply system could not sustain a new effort. It must have been with great reluctance that he abandoned his third successive failure on 18 June and withdrew his divisions to their base areas. The withdrawal across the Day River was very difficult for the Viet Minh because of the French landing craft patrols, and several hundred prisoners were taken. Not all of these prisoners resented their capture, for disillusionment had begun to grow within Viet Minh ranks. The increasing emphasis being placed on Communist doctrines, and the tightening of controls, led many nationalists to leave the Viet Minh in 1951 to work in the French-held areas for a non-Communist but independent Vietnamese state. Several thousand members of the three attacking divisions became battle casualties. Even had Giap not drawn the lessons of these three failures, the state of his army would have permitted no fourth attempt on the delta in 1951.

By July 1951 the Viet Minh had lost over 20,000 killed and wounded as a result of the delta battles. Giap had held the initiative at the beginning of the year, but had lost it within six months. He now had to withdraw into his safe areas, re-think his approach to the war, and restore the fighting strength of his army to its former state. During this time he would have to be on his guard against a jubilant de Lattre seeking to exploit his opponent's moment of weakness. It was fortunate for the Viet Minh that the French lacked the strength for a major offensive. Unless French policy was radically changed in Paris or unless the Americans diverted some of their resources from the Korean War, the French were obliged to remain on the strategic defensive, so that Giap was able to attempt another solution. The only problem for him was how. If he could not find more vulnerable points in the French dispositions, he might wear out the Viet Minh strength in futile attacks, while the French remained in control of the two vital regions of Vietnam. Giap must have realized that unless he could produce some good new ideas during the wet season of 1951, the Viet Minh cause stood in grave danger either of impotence or of a challenge from the non-Communist nationalists. While Viet Minh strength and organizational techniques together with Chinese support would have been sufficient to offset these threats in the long term, the revolutionary movement could have faced a setback of several years. Giap was approaching his most testing few months as a strategist.

6 Winning Back the Initiative

The triple failure of the Red River delta offensive provoked intense self-analysis on the part of the Viet Minh High Command. Not only had the collapse of Viet Minh morale to be countered and the army re-formed, but also a better plan for the direction of the war in the coming year had to be evolved. The main force units withdrew into the Viet Bac for re-training, re-equipment and the induction of reinforcements. Regional force activity slackened and the guerrillas in the delta lay low while a new policy was being formulated. Obviously, the Viet Minh could not hope to regain the initiative by a repetition of the strategy of the previous campaign season but French exploitation of their success had to be minimized by striking hard whenever the French manoeuvred into a vulnerable position.

Events in South Vietnam had also been causing acute concern to Ho Chi Minh and Giap. The Nationalist resistance to the French in Cochin China had been broken into many rival groups at the end of 1945 and a new leader, Nguyen Phong Thao or Nguyen Binh, was sent by Ho Chi Minh to restore the situation.[10]

[10]This information may be found in *Ai Giet Trung Tuong Nguyen Binh* *(Who Killed Major General Nguyen Binh)*, by Thai Lan (Saigon, 1960).
    The name Thai Lan suggests a pen name chosen by a Vietnamese returning from Thailand. The Vietnamese in exile in Thailand sent two battalions, later to become two regiments, *Cuu Long* I and II (*Cuu Long* is Vietnamese

Nguyen Binh was born in 1904 in the Red River delta province of Hung Yen. He became a teacher and commenced revolutionary activities in 1923, joining the VNQDD under Nguyen Thai Hoc. The latter asked Nguyen Binh to go to Cochin China to establish the southern branch of the VNQDD in 1925. As leader of the VNQDD in Cochin China, he was arrested after the abortive Yen Bay uprisings of 1930 and imprisoned on Poulo Condore where he met several leading Communists. The French Popular Front government released him in 1936 and he went to sea in the S.S. *Athos* which worked between France and China, before entering the Whampoa Military Academy in South China. In 1945 he re-entered Tonkin and established the Fourth Military Region which covered the area between Hon Gay and Mon Cay. By the time of the Japanese surrender, Nguyen Binh was the undisputed nationalist leader of this region.

After Ho Chi Minh had been installed in Hanoi, he wrote to Nguyen Binh:

My Dear Binh,
The South needs a strategist to lead the Resistance. I am confident that you have the ability and so I have proposed you for the South. I hope that you succeed.

Nguyen Binh was replaced by Hoang Van Thai who later became Chief of the Viet Minh General Staff. Affairs in the South were in a serious condition when Nguyen Binh arrived because the local war lords had been expending their energies in pursuing personal vendettas, piracy, pillage and rape. He brought the situation under control gradually through setting up military courts to punish these offenders, through winning the allegiance of Le Van Vien, alias Bay Vien, and his river pirates, the *Binh Xuyen*, and through building a command structure for directing guerrilla warfare. Fifteen battalion-sized units were raised and placed under three zone head-

---

for Mekong) to the South. Thai Lan acknowledges his story to a certain V.V.D. who served close to Nguyen Binh and hence establishes a claim to authenticity. This claim has been supported by a friend of the author who knew various of Nguyen Binh's assistants who were named by Thai Lan when he was in the Fourth Military Region in 1945.

quarters for Cochin China. The first zone, in the east, was commanded by Nguyen Binh, his deputy being Bay Vien. The other zones were commanded by Tran Van Tra and Huynh Phan Ho.

These battalions were expanded on the orders of Le Duan in the North to form twenty-two regiments, of which eleven were under the command of Nguyen Binh. Growing VNQDD opposition to Binh for his transfer of affection to the Communists resulted in an attempt on his life in July 1947. While he was being nursed back to health after severe wounding, Binh was placed in the care of a Viet Minh female cadre, Vuong Thi Trinh, who persuaded him to join the Communist Party. After promotion to Major General in January 1948, Binh was called on by the Party to carry out increasingly hazardous tasks, while Party control over his actions grew even tighter. Le Duc Tho and Duong Quoc Chinh were sent to the South to organize a central headquarters for direction of the military-political struggle, an administrative committee under Le Duan, and a military headquarters in which the military component was commanded by Binh and Duong Quoc Chinh and the political members by Pham Ngoc Thuan.

In June 1948 Bay Vien took the *Binh Xuyen* out of the Resistance to support the Cochin Chinese separatist premier, General Xuan, and during the following year Nguyen Binh lost effective control of his army. After the failure of the 1950 offensives against Saigon and Can Tho, Binh was made the scapegoat and was summoned to Tonkin. Duong Quoc Chinh re-organized the South in Binh's place while Le Duan took over from Pham Ngoc Thuan.

Binh's summons to the North was virtually a death sentence. Ho wished this to be carried out far away from Binh's followers and in such a way as to appear accidental. Binh commenced the arduous journey in very poor health and in the company of a Viet Minh assassin. Warning of his route had been given to French-Cambodian troops in his path and he was killed by the assassin during a clash with these troops near Phum Sre Pok in Stung Treng Province on 27 October 1951.

This is only one of many cases in which the Viet Minh exploited and eliminated non-Communist leaders devoted to the national cause.

Giap, who had played a leading role in the fall of Nguyen Binh, was now in much greater control of events in the South, and although still consolidating his position in the North, he had demonstrated the strength of his intolerance of independent subordinates.

The French—despite their successes, improved morale, and dashing commander—were not in a position to follow up their victories over Giap and pursue his forces into the mountains. While they were strong around the edges of the Red River delta, they were tied down too fully to be able to spare the divisions which an effective attack on the Viet Bac required. Furthermore, although Giap had conceded defeat, he had lived to fight another day and so had the bulk of his forces. Although the battles around the delta had shown that the Viet Minh were not strong enough to break through the de Lattre line, the French had not regained any territory and the resources of Tonkin outside the delta, both human and otherwise, were sufficiently intact to enable Giap to recoup his losses and restore the balance of power in Indo China to the state of late 1950. In these circumstances, what could the French have done?

Most perceptive observers of the scene in mid-1951 must have realized that the French did not have the military strength to annihilate the Viet Minh. Therefore, if they could not be destroyed, they would have to be negotiated with and the negotiations made from the strongest position which the French could achieve. The growing American presence in East Asia as a result of the Korean War encouraged de Lattre to think that if he could obtain massive deliveries of arms and equipment, together with a large sum of money to increase the Vietnamese National Army, he could put Giap in a much weaker position. If the bait were made attractive enough, de Lattre might even have hoped to lure Giap into further defeats which would seriously damage the image of the Viet Minh.

The field of choice confronting de Lattre was not wide. He had to mount an operation sufficiently provocative to draw Giap into the attack, yet he had to keep close to the main position around the delta if his limited forces were to have a chance of success once Giap had joined battle. The only type of operation which fulfilled these basic requirements was a short thrust out from the delta to take one of the several towns which lay within thirty or forty miles of the French perimeter. Going further afield would have endangered the French lines of communication too much, while a more modest operation would have been unlikely to have achieved anything more than a lengthening of the de Lattre line and the creation of new defence problems.

Possibly sensing that these thoughts were occupying de Lattre's mind, Giap launched a thrust against one of the key French outposts in the hills between the Red and Black Rivers. 312 Division crossed the Red River in late September and launched a number of attacks on Nghia Lo in early October. French paratroops were dropped in to the post in numbers sufficient to withstand the attacks. Perhaps this diversion of French resources had been Giap's purpose. He withdrew his troops, not wishing to repeat one of his earlier defeats through attacking French defensive positions too strongly, and began to plan his activities for the coming season of dry weather.

He had progressed far with his thinking when it was his turn to be diverted by de Lattre. The French Commander had just returned from a visit to the U.S.A. to press his claims for support in the war against Communism. He was well aware of the need for demonstrating that the French Army was worth supporting, both to the American Congress and to the French National Assembly which was about to debate the budget for operations in Indo China in the coming financial year. Giap's withdrawal to the north bank of the Red River seemed to offer a good chance for launching a thrust before the Viet Minh army was able to redispose its forces. There were three towns within forty miles of the French perimeter from which de Lattre could choose his target: Thanh Hoa in the south, Hoa

Binh in the west and Thai Nguyen in the north. Thanh Hoa
was an important Viet Minh stronghold and around it was
based 320 Division. However, seizure of Thanh Hoa would
not have weakened this division seriously, since a great part
of its supplies came from the Viet Bac via a track system which
passed around the Red River delta through Hoa Binh.

A blow at Hoa Binh therefore offered the advantage of cutting an important Viet Minh supply link, and because the
town was on the west bank of the Black River near its exit
from the mountains, an operation against Hoa Binh could be
supplied both over land and by water, making the passage of
heavy stores for the French much easier. Thai Nguyen, on the
southern edge of the Viet Bac, was very close to Giap's main
force units and to his bases. An operation in this direction
could have been very costly for de Lattre. Perhaps the most
important difference between Hoa Binh on the one hand and
Thanh Hoa and Thai Nguyen on the other was in the attitudes
of the local people towards the opposing sides, for while the
people of Thanh Hoa and Thai Nguyen had been predominantly Viet Minh supporters for several years, the Muongs,
whose capital was at Hoa Binh, favoured the French. Thus the
seizure of Hoa Binh would not only offer fewer difficulties to
the French but it would be an important psychological blow
against the Viet Minh in an area in which they were weak.

Giap's reaction to the French parachute landing at Hoa
Binh on 14 November 1951 was one of caution. The Viet
Minh independent regiment in the area did not offer any great
resistance to the French, contenting themselves with observation of the attackers, reporting their strength to the High Command in the Viet Bac. Giap weighed the situation and con-
ferred with the other members of the Central Committee so
that any action taken against the French at Hoa Binh became
a matter of collective rather than individual responsibility. The
threat which the French move had posed to the Viet Minh
supply line was not one to be easily ignored by the Viet Minh
military leaders. The political leaders, who in several cases
were also the military leaders, saw the French seizure of the

Muong capital as a significant blow to Viet Minh popular strength if no counter action was taken, and so Giap was entrusted with the conduct of an operation aimed at defeating de Lattre's new initiative.

The battles of the first months of the year had taught Giap the dangers of concentrating large numbers of troops in areas which could be bombarded by the French Air Force. He needed several divisions to cope with the numbers of French

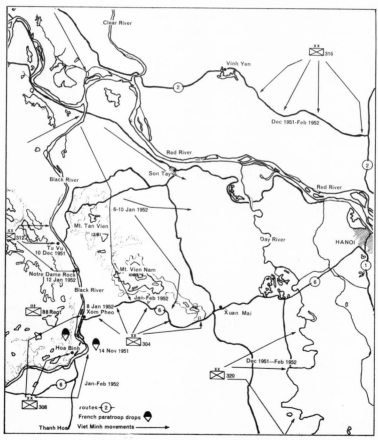

Giap's Strategy to Counter the Hoa Binh Offensive of de Lattre,
14 November 1951—24 February 1952

troops protecting Hoa Binh and its approaches, but these divisions were ordered to spread out and harass the French at many points. 304 Division moved in close to the southern side of Route 6, 308 Division positioned itself around Hoa Binh, leaving only the north-eastern sector open to French traffic via the Black River and Route 6. 312 Division closed in along the west bank of the Black River between Hoa Binh and the confluence of the Red and Black Rivers, thirty miles north of Hoa Binh. 316 Division participated directly in the Hoa Binh battle by remaining along the northern side of the de Lattre Line with the task of penetrating the French perimeter to draw off reserves from Hoa Binh and to harass the supply lines running to the Black River. 320 Division was given a similar role, namely to penetrate the de Lattre Line on the Day River sector and to create confusion in the French rear areas.

These dispositions show a strategic skill which Giap had not evidenced in previous operations. Scorning to make a direct attack on the well defended French position around Hoa Binh, he decided to concentrate his weight on the supply lines, the Black River and Route 6. However before the degree of credit due to Giap for this change of approach can be assessed, it is relevant to examine the ground around the Hoa Binh salient.

The airstrip at Hoa Binh lay to the north of the town and both were situated on a flat spit which forced the Black River to make a right angle bend around it to the east. This spit was overlooked by hills several hundred feet high on either side. To the east, jungle clad hills rose steeply from the Black River, and to the west the jungle began right by Hoa Binh, covering the long slopes which ascended to a crest line some three miles from the town. Thus both the town and the airstrip were under constant Viet Minh surveillance and the latter was vulnerable to Viet Minh artillery.

To the north of Hoa Binh the hills closed in on the Black River making a narrow valley over twenty miles in length which could be controlled by sniper fire from the hillsides.

Because of the poor standard of Route 6, the Black River was extremely important for the maintenance of the Hoa Binh garrison. Consequently the French were compelled to station some thousands of men along the river to keep the Viet Minh out of the valley. These men occupied a chain of tiny posts facing a vast uncontrolled hinterland in which the Viet Minh could move and concentrate, taking out the French posts one at a time. The west bank of the Black River was no place to build another de Lattre line.

Route 6 had been sabotaged by the Viet Minh some years previously and a major French engineering effort was required to restore it to a road capable of bearing heavy vehicles. The road wound through twenty miles of hills between the edge of the delta at Xuan Mai and the Black River and presented problems of defence. The triangle between the de Lattre line, Route 6 and the Black River was also hilly. Dominated by two mountains over three thousand feet high, Tan Vien and Vien Nam, it provided refuge for small parties of Viet Minh, enabling Giap to conduct operations against both sides of the French lines of communications.

Had Giap ignored these tactical advantages over the French supply system, his ability would have been of a very low order. Once he had realized where his strength lay, it did not take him long to discomfort the French severely. He opened his battle by a series of attacks on the most vulnerable part of the French lines, the Black River. 308 and 312 Divisions launched overpowering attacks on French outposts isolated from their rear support areas by the Black River. Heavy French counter attacks found nothing, because these two divisions had orders to fight only when they enjoyed unquestionable superiority. The weight of the Viet Minh attack shifted to the Hoa Binh basin and to Route 6 in early January 1952, but continuous pressure was maintained along the Black River line. The new French commander, General Salan (who had taken over from de Lattre when the latter became fatally stricken by cancer) was forced by this pressure to with-

draw from the west bank. The passage of river convoys soon
became too hazardous to attempt in the face of Viet Minh
rockets and artillery being fired from the water's edge, and by
mid-January the battle had shifted to Route 6.

Similar tactics forced Salan to concede that the operation
was not worth the French casualties entailed in attempts to
supply the Hoa Binh garrison. The airstrip had been pounded
by mortar fire, and aircraft on their confined approach run
had become the prey of anti-aircraft batteries up in the hills
to the west. Had Giap closed Route 6, the French position in
Hoa Binh would have been untenable. 304 and 308 Divisions
set about this final task while the Black River line was being
evacuated. Stubborn French defence made this operation a
costly one for the Viet Minh but nonetheless they cut the road
so effectively that it took a force of twelve battalions to re-open
it. The huge number of French troops required to maintain
control of the road had drained off many of the delta reserves
which were being called on to stem the waves of infiltration
launched by 316 and 320 Divisions. On 22 February 1952 the
humiliating French withdrawal from Hoa Binh began.

Persistent attacks by the Viet Minh made the withdrawal a
constant running battle which lasted two days. When the final
French losses were reckoned up after the Hoa Binh offensive,
they amounted to several thousand. Their failure to avoid
defeat in an operation of this size boded ill for any larger
thrusts. In effect, French capacity for offensive operations
beyond the Red River delta in Tonkin had become whittled
away to vanishing point. However, the French politicians were
unable to accept the conclusion to be drawn from their
military impotence in Indo China, and the French Army had
to fight on.

Giap doubtless realized this, and deduced that if the French
Army was going to keep fighting hard, it might be possible to
lure more of it out from behind the defences of the delta into
wild territory where Giap might even have been able to
weaken the French sufficiently to force a political settlement
of the war on Viet Minh terms. His major strategic problem in

early 1952 was one of logistics—how to supply troops operating at great distances from their bases, in country where even
an unladen man found the going difficult. His first measure
was to establish supply points as far forward as possible and to
fill them with materials from China, carried in Soviet trucks
and by Vietnamese porters. The next move was to recruit new
armies of porters from the whole of Tonkin so that he had a
high degree of flexibility concerning the selection of areas in
which he could operate.

Having overcome the limitations of his earlier supply
system, Giap was free to consider the most profitable direction
to take in order to cause maximum losses to the French in
terms of casualties, of territory and people under their control,
and of public confidence in the ability of the French to avoid
defeat in Indo China. Excluding the Red River delta, there
were four main areas into which Giap could send his main
force—Central Vietnam, South Vietnam, Cambodia and Laos
—and he had the choice of operating in any one or in several
of these areas, at once. Cambodia offered the least prospects
of success, for not only were Vietnamese of any political shade
regarded as traditional aggressors by the Cambodians but the
Cambodian Government had carried out a most effective
resettlement programme which had severed the population
from the insurgents, thereby removing some of the essential
pre-conditions for guerrilla warfare—local resources of man-
power, food and intelligence.

The densely populated Mekong delta lacked the disadvantage of differing nationality, but the openness of the countryside and the high quality of the major communications routes
placed the French in a strong position with regard to the Viet
Minh. The collapse of the 1950 revolt in the South which
Nguyen Binh had led complicated matters for Giap, so that it
was thought inadvisable to attempt the long journey to Cochin
China for the sake of the revolution. In Central Vietnam, the
ruggedness of the country and the poor standard of communications had placed the French in a most vulnerable position—
holding several outposts linked only by narrow roads which

wound through gorges and jungles. Ambush sites abounded, and the limitations on what the French Air Force could carry compelled the Army to depend on the roads for supplies and for troop movement. Consequently Central Vietnam had much to offer Giap as a possible theatre of operations.

The fourth area, Laos, also suffered from the Cambodian disadvantage of a differing nationality. However, there was a sufficient degree of overlap between the hill tribes in western Tonkin and eastern Laos to make this difference of minor importance only. Perhaps the greatest advantage which Laos had to offer Giap was the weak and superficial nature of French control. Apart from the main towns in the Mekong valley, such as Vientiane, Luang Prabang, Thakkek and Seno, the French had garrisons only at widely scattered points such as Phong Saly, Muong Khoua, Sam Neua and Xieng Khouang. Most of these garrisons were very difficult to reach from the Mekong valley, and roads which came through from Tonkin were few. These posts could be attacked singly, surrounded, or merely by-passed by Giap's divisions. Because Laos was the only Indo Chinese state which looked upon the French Union with favour, its defence was important to the French, so that a Viet Minh thrust towards the Mekong towns could not be ignored by Salan.

Giap was probably well aware that the French commander would try to halt a Viet Minh drive into Laos by determined forward action in the mountains of north-west Tonkin, south of the Black River. This area was as far removed from the main French bases as any in Indo China could be, so that Giap would be fighting the French at their weakest in these mountains. From Giap's point of view, operations in north-west Tonkin posed fewer problems of logistics than in any of the other areas. In threatening the French at their weakest point, then, he was engaging them at his strongest. As a good general, he had no need to look further than this for the basis of his strategy during the coming campaign season.

On 11 October 1952, three Viet Minh divisions crossed the Red River and began to work forward to the French outposts between the Red and Black Rivers. 312 Division formed the right flank, 316 Division the left, and 308 Division was the central element of the advance. 148 Independent Regiment swept around in a wide arc to the north of the main force divisions. 308 and 316 Divisions had each left one regiment behind to secure the forward bases and river crossings around Yen Bay. Six days later, 308 Division emerged from the jungle to launch a heavy attack on the main French post of Nghia Lo, taking it in a night. Desperate French commitment of paratroops enabled several of the garrisons of other posts to make the punishing withdrawal to the south bank of the Black River, but by early November, Giap's spearheads had also reached the river.

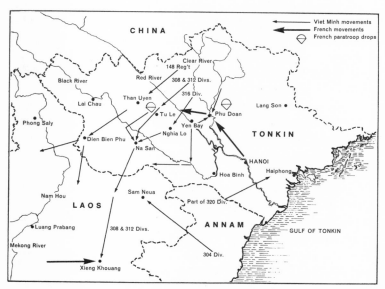

Giap's Offensive in North-West Tonkin, 1952-53

Salan ordered the preparation of a major defensive position at Na San, fifteen miles south-west of the Black River line, and on the main axis of the Viet Minh line of advance. More than a division of French troops were flown into Na San, and quickly spread out to occupy a defensive perimeter on the low hilltops which surrounded the airfield. The Viet Minh divisions were beginning to outrun their supply system, having advanced seventy miles across fearful country in three weeks, and so Giap ordered a halt while their food and ammunition trains of porters caught up.

While pressure on the French defences south of the Black River was beginning to ease, Salan was planning a counter attack. He reasoned that Giap's most vulnerable point was his supply system, and that since the bulk of the Viet Minh main force was across the Black River, the time was ripe for a blow against the forward bases north-east of the Red River around Yen Bay. *Operation Lorraine* began on 29 October with a thrust from the north-west corner of the de Lattre line towards Phu Tho. The speed of the French mechanized advance caught some of Giap's rear units by surprise, so that Phu Doan, a small town crammed with Viet Minh war material, was captured on 9 November. Further to the north-west, more large arms dumps were found, including Soviet-made *Molotova* trucks and machine guns.

After these initial successes, it was not to be expected that the Viet Minh would be caught napping in other base areas. General Salan had no mobile reserves for the vital delta region while *Operation Lorraine* was in progress, so on 14 November he ordered his troops to withdraw into the security of the de Lattre line. During the past week, the Viet Minh local commanders had been planning a devastating blow to be delivered against the inevitable French withdrawal which, they well knew, would have to use the main road, Route 2. This road threaded its way through the Chan Muong valley whose steep sides—cliffs in places—were only a few hundred yards apart. The three-mile length of the valley was sufficient to trap several French units at the one time

The two main force regiments left behind to protect the base areas quickly moved to cover the Chan Muong valley in readiness for an ambush when the French were making their withdrawal. On 17 November, the French began to pass through the valley, and having no alternative route, were forced to fight their way through an ambush of regimental size, at a cost of over three hundred casualties. Seven days later, this ambush was followed up by an attack on the French rear guard before it had withdrawn across the Clear River. By 1 December 1952, *Operation Lorraine* was finished; the French had suffered over five hundred casualties in return for insufficient quantities of Viet Minh supplies to halt the advance towards Laos.

While the French were painfully fighting their way back to the Red River delta along Route 2, the defences of Na San had been severely battered. 308 Division launched a heavy attack on the evening of 23 November, penetrating the outer perimeter but failing to make any permanent inroads. A week later, another attack was mounted, lasting through two nights, and meeting with similar results. Over one thousand Viet Minh dead were found around the French perimeter after these attacks, and probably Giap had lost over half of the division through casualties. The most likely explanation for Giap's miscalculation in pressing these attacks is poor intelligence, for at Na San he was operating beyond the boundary of the 'liberated area'.

The effort of these attacks drained the Viet Minh supply system for several weeks, and 308 Division withdrew from the Na San area, leaving one regiment to mask the French garrison and to prevent it from making forays against the main advance. Giap learned that he would have to seek even greater natural advantages if he was to compete successfully with French fire and air power in a set-piece battle in north-west Tonkin. Unfortunately for the French, their High Command seemed to be misled by the success of the defence of Na San into the over-confident notion that they could challenge Giap with impunity from a divisional sized fortress anywhere in Tonkin. Those who had participated in the defence of Na San and who had experienced what a near thing it had been for the French knew better, but their voices were not clearly heard in the quiet of the map rooms in Saigon and Hanoi.

During 1952 the French began to employ considerable

numbers of irregular troops to strike at Giap's rear areas and
force him into the same over-commitment which the French
faced. Known as *Groupement de Commandos Mixtes Aero-
portes* or GCMAs these groups were based on the T'ai mountain tribes, who disliked the imposition of a new way of life by
strangers from the coastal plains. Their numbers varied from
small squads to battalion strength units under the leadership of
French senior non-commissioned officers or, occasionally, a
lieutenant. The problems of winning and retaining the confidence of the tribesmen were not simple to overcome and
required a great deal of patience and tolerance in the scrupu-
lous observance of local taboos and customs. The task of the
GCMA leaders was made even more arduous by the complete
lack of recognition shown towards their valour in terms of
decorations and promotion. It seems miraculous that they per-
severed when faced with an indeterminate period beyond the
security of a French perimeter, their safety in the hands of
tribesmen amongst whom a Viet Minh assassin could have
infiltrated.

The men of the GCMAs overcame their difficulties sufficiently well to pose a considerable nuisance to Giap. Unfortunately the French had been too late in developing this new
concept of warfare to cause severe disruption to the Viet Minh
but the fifteen thousand men who made up the irregular forces
tied down many more Viet Minh than had been possible for
the conventional units. The GCMAs set up a number of bases
in the most remote parts of the Tonkin mountains, usually in
the vicinity of a rough landing strip which would take the
smallest *Morane* scout aircraft. In 1954 a few helicopters became available and these greatly increased the support available to the irregulars, but usually when a man was wounded in
a clash, he had to be carried over wild jungle paths for days to
elude the determined Viet Minh pursuit.

The major GCMA bases were at Lai Chau on the Black
River in the far west of Tonkin, in the mountains around Fan
Si Pan, the highest mountain in Tonkin and a little to the south
of Lao Kay on the Red River, and in the border country

A Viet Minh guerrilla in jungle camouflage —*Vietnam Peoples Army*

Bridge destroyed by Viet Minh guerrillas

Viet Minh hauling a Chinese field gun into position to bombard French forces at Dien Bien Phu

Bicycle transport behind the Viet Minh lines
—*Vietnam Peoples Army*

General Giap at his Command Post in the mountains near Dien Bien Phu
—*Vietnam Peoples Army*

The fall of Dien Bien Phu—10.000 French prisoners
—*Vietnam Peoples Army*

Top left: Viet Minh troops crossing Muong Thanh bridge
for the last attack on Dien Bien Phu
—*Vietnam Peoples Army*

Left: Viet Minh soldiers hoist their flag atop de Castries' bunker
—*Vietnam Peoples Army*

A general view of Dien Bien Phu just after the French surrender

French liaison officers escort the first Viet Minh troops entering the French lines in August 1954

—*Vietnam Peoples Army*

Victory parade of Viet Minh artillery units in Hanoi

—*Vietnam Peoples Army*

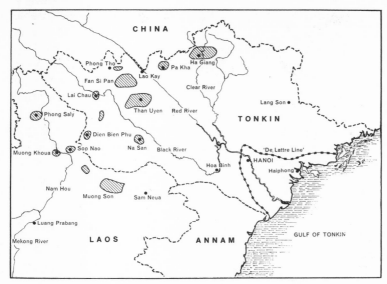

The Secret War—French Irregular Forces, 1953-54

between Pa Kha and Ha Giang. Viet Minh resources were not sufficient to mount large-scale operations to flush the French-led tribesmen out of their mountains and so they were able to maintain a perilous existence which in at least one case extended until 1959, five years after the Geneva cease fire. Raids against Viet Minh supply points gradually increased until in 1953, six hundred tribesmen attacked Ho-K'ou, the Chinese town opposite Lao Kay, where they destroyed significant amounts of Viet Minh stores. Giap's subordinate commanders began to feel the shortages of supplies due to these raids sufficiently to be seriously worried by them. Another French gain from these operations resulted from Viet Minh loss of face among the mountain people who witnessed the effectiveness of the GCMAs.

Giap was never able to rid himself of these irregular groups, and by 1954 at least ten Viet Minh battalions were tied down in routine security duties, protecting supply dumps and routes and in pursuit of the elusive raiders. Such an achievement at the height of the Dien Bien Phu battle imposed a considerable strain on Giap's reinforcement system for the main conflict. A measure of the effectiveness of the GCMAs has been given by one of their commanders thus: the 5,000 members of GCMAs operating in western Tonkin and north-eastern Laos during the Dien Bien Phu battle immobilized up to fourteen Viet Minh battalions for a cost of 200 tons of supplies per month while the 15,000 men in the Dien Bien Phu fortifications engaged twenty-eight battalions at a cost of 200 tons of supplies per day.[11] However, it is to Giap's credit that the GCMAs were not permitted to make any serious attack on the vital supply routes between the Viet Bac and Dien Bien Phu, but how many security forces were required to prevent such attacks will never be known, unless Giap returns to the role of historian.

After 308 Division had drawn back from Na San and the small French garrison had been ejected from the Dien Bien Phu valley, Giap paused for a few months, marshalling and supplying his forces in the mountains within twenty miles of the Laotian border. Clearly no French strong points lay in his path within Tonkin and he was free to plan the entry into Laos while the French endeavoured to obstruct him. The towns in the Mekong valley were very poorly defended and the whole French position in Laos was clearly menaced. Giap had no need to hasten, because his divisions were out of range of French attacks by land, and the rugged country so impeded the Air Force that French bombing could be faced with equanimity. Had Giap been too impatient, his Tonkin offensive might have outrun its strength long before it had approached its goal.

While they remained in the hills near the Laotian border, Giap's divisions could threaten the French at several points— the delta, Na San, Lai Chau, and generally throughout Laos. Until the weight of his next thrust was felt by the French, they could not know which eventuality to meet. The initial onslaught was not sufficient indication, for it might have been

[11]Col. Roger Trinquier, *Modern Warfare: a French View of Counterinsurgency* (Frederick A. Praeger, New York, 1964).

only a feint. Thus, while Giap's forces were regaining their full strength and energy, the French were wearing themselves out with furious preparations throughout the whole of their northern domain. By 1953 Giap's strategy had reached a degree of sophistication and elegance which was remarkable by comparison with his generalship in 1951.

By early April 1953 he was ready, and on 9 April his troops moved forward into Laos. Several French outposts were ordered to fight to the last in a pattern of delaying actions while the Royal elephants dragged logs into position to defend Luang Prabang. The advance moved on three axes to permit maximum flexibility and to offer the best chances for rapid dispersal in the event of heavy air attacks. The left thrust passed through Sam Neua, then swung in towards the centre to halt before the main French fortification on the Plain of Jars, Jars Camp, which blocked the route to Vientiane. In the centre, another drive went down the Nam Seng valley and on the right a third force made its way down the main communications artery, the Nam Hou, until it reached the strongly defended outpost of Muong Khoua. After some delay, two regiments remained to wear down Muong Khoua while another two went on down the Nam Hou to link up with the central thrust some thirty miles north of Luang Prabang. The central force then swung away to the south-east while the two regiments which had come down the Nam Hou valley forced in the French outposts around Luang Prabang and then invested the Royal capital.

The camp on the Plain of Jars had been skilfully sited by Salan to threaten the approach from Luang Prabang to Vientiane as well as the road from Xieng Khouang. The central and left flank forces combined and encircled the Jars Camp. The French in Laos were then confined to several small areas which could be supplied only by air while the Viet Minh controlled the northern countryside—a poor position for Salan to be in at the beginning of the wet season. After the rains had set in, Giap's supply problems increased to the point at which he felt that continued maintenance of his divisions in Laos was counter productive and in early May he withdrew most of his forces to Tonkin where they could be more easily supplied. His thrust into Laos was over and the French were able to come out of their fortifications and move about the country again.

This quiet ending to Giap's most dramatic offensive may seem something of an anti-climax, but his readiness to withdraw from what was becoming a difficult situation showed once again that he had acquired great poise as a strategist. He realized that the loss of face involved in ordering his troops to withdraw from territory that they had just fought to gain was insignificant beside the possibilities which the next campaign season offered if his army were in good condition, rested, re-supplied and re-organized. After all, control of the Laotian jungles did not represent very much of a gain in itself, while a clear demonstration of his capacity to move at will in north-ern Laos achieved just as great a psychological effect on the inhabitants of the French controlled towns as if Giap had all his forces besieging their walls. Furthermore, in making his withdrawal from Laos, Giap may have hoped to have laid the foundation for a major victory over the French in the follow-ing year, because they then had the whole of the wet season to recover, plan and prepare what might be a desperate gamble to provide for the security of Laos. Had he not withdrawn, French boldness may have given way to caution, leaving Giap in undisputed control of thousands of square miles of sparsely populated, jungle-covered mountains while the French remained securely in control of the major cities—the real objects of the war.

7 The Navarre Plan

The strategies adopted by both the French and the Viet Minh at Dien Bien Phu have given rise to so much conflicting comment and confusion that it is necessary to examine in detail the intentions of the two opponents before a sound appraisal of Giap's conduct of the battle can be made. Viet Minh reactions to the French occupation of the remote mountain valley cannot be assessed correctly without knowledge of the French aims and of the changes in these aims which were forced on the French by the various limitations under which they were operating. Hence it is important to examine the origins of Dien Bien Phu in the thinking of the French High Command and to trace the evolution of the plan which led to the stationing of 16,000 men there.

Because Dien Bien Phu is situated in a valley amongst a tangle of mountains over 150 miles across, there is a tendency to think of it as simply an insignificant, isolated village among thousands of others, with no great strategic importance, and to think that therefore the French were stupid to commit such large numbers to the defence of a post which could not exercise much influence over the course of the war. However this was not the way in which those who knew Tonkin regarded Dien Bien Phu, and its importance has been summed up best by Giap himself, thus:

Dien Bien Phu is a large plain 18 kilometres long and six to
eight kilometres wide in the mountainous zone of the North-
West. It is the biggest and richest of the four plains in this hilly
region close to the Viet Nam-Laos frontier. It is situated at the
junction of important roads, running to the North-East towards
Lai Chau, to the East and South-East towards Tuan Giao, Son
La, Na San; to the West towards Luang Prabang and to the
South towards Sam Neua. In the theatre of operations of Bac Bo
[i.e. Tonkin] and Upper Laos, Dien Bien Phu is a strategic
position of first importance, capable of becoming an infantry and
air base of extreme efficiency.[12]

Dien Bien Phu had been taken out of French hands in late
1952 by Giap's 316 Division who, with 148 Independent
Regiment, had forced their way through from the Red River.
The French Commander in Chief, General Salan, regarded
this loss as serious, largely because of the access routes into
Laos which were now under Viet Minh control. On 30
December 1952 he issued Directive No. 40 ordering a counter
attack for 10 January 1953 and stating:

> The reoccupation of Dien Bien Phu must constitute in the forth-
> coming period the first step for the regaining of control of the
> T'ai country and for the elimination of the Viet Minh from the
> area west of the Black River.[13]

Other commitments prevented Salan from making this
counter attack, but before he was relieved by General Henri
Navarre in May, he stressed the importance of Dien Bien Phu
in two memoranda to the Minister for Associated States, Jean
Letourneau.

Navarre was a strange choice for this crucial post, because
he had no previous experience of operations in Indo China.
However he had coped with a widely differing number of
situations in his earlier career, from the trenches of the Western

[12]Vo Nguyen Giap, *People's War People's Army* (Foreign Languages
Publishing House, Hanoi, 1961, p. 206 (Frederick A. Praeger, New York,
1962).
[13]*Directive No. 40* of 30 December 1952, *803/EMIFT/TS*, cited in
Bernard Fall, *Hell in a Very Small Place* (J. B. Lippincott, Philadelphia,
1966), p. 25

Front in 1917-8, to anti-guerrilla operations in Syria and Algeria between the wars, senior intelligence appointments and command of an armoured regiment during the thrust into Germany in 1945, and so there were grounds for hoping that he would not be defeated by the environmental factors in Indo China. He came to Saigon to assume his appointment some-what unwillingly, but since he had not been prepared to resign over the issue, he had made the best of it.

Several of the senior commanders in Indo China were due for relief, as their terms of duty were expiring, and Navarre had the advantage of being able personally to select his chief lieutenants. For the most vital sector, Tonkin, he chose the commander of the Second Infantry Division, Brigadier General René Cogny, against the advice of Cogny's prede-cessor, General de Linares. Cogny had the reputation of being an argumentative subordinate with a thin skin and once his pride was wounded he would fight whoever he thought respon-sible. He was a brilliant man however, with a diploma in political science and a doctorate in jurisprudence, so that Giap was not the only general of the Indo China War with high academic qualifications.

Navarre spent the first three weeks of his period in Indo China in a series of inspection tours which took him to every part of the country, sometimes at considerable personal risk. Perhaps the most significant place which Navarre visited was the fortified camp at Na San. Not only was Navarre brought face to face with a successful new idea, but he made the acquaintance of a man who was later to play an important role in the planning of the Dien Bien Phu operation—Colonel Berteil. Navarre was looking for ideas, and the combination of the marginal success of Na San and the extraordinary eloquence of Berteil in describing the camp in terms of intricate strategic theories, led Navarre into the error of think-ing that Na San contained the seed of a new method for defeat-ing the Viet Minh. Navarre was also sufficiently impressed by Berteil to have him re-posted to Saigon as his deputy chief of staff for operations. Those who understood the reasons behind

Berteil's new appointment began to lay wagers on where the
next Na San would be situated.

After considering the experiences of his tour Navarre assembled his regional commanders in Saigon on 16 June 1953, and
expounded his formula for inflicting the maximum damage on
the Viet Minh in the coming campaign season. His plan consisted of five points:

   reconstruction of the Expeditionary Force during a period
   of restrained activity,
   a major pacification action in the Red River delta,
   the destruction of the Viet Minh in the Southern Highlands
   by means of *Operation Atlante,*
   prevention of Viet Minh offensives by smashing them before
   they were launched, and
   a quest for a major set piece battle, attacking Giap's rice
   granaries, reserves of men, and finally the main Viet Minh
   battle force.

Part of this plan required the evacuation of Na San which
was envisaged for August 1953. As it stood, it seems a reasonable enough programme. The French troops needed a period
in which to recuperate, the Red River delta needed some attention, the Viet Minh in the Southern Highlands could be attacked by an amphibious operation in overwhelming strength and,
once this foundation had been laid, the Expeditionary Force
would have been free to harass the Viet Minh main forces.
However, there were dangers in the timing and in the location
of this final phase. If it were launched before the French Army
was ready it could lead swiftly to a new over-commitment of
Navarre's resources, and if battle were sought on unfavourable
ground, the outcome could be defeat not of the Viet Minh
but of the French.

At this stage, Dien Bien Phu did not feature prominently in
Navarre's plans and it seems likely that he had no formed intention of giving effect to Salan's Directive No. 40. However,
either at this conference or shortly afterwards, Cogny sug-
gested to Navarre that it would be a good idea to set up a base
or mooring point for carrying guerrilla warfare into Giap's

rear should he decide to re-new his drive on Laos. A natural location for this mooring point would be Dien Bien Phu. It should be noted that this concept of a mooring point was vastly different from that of a fortified camp which was intended to withstand a long siege mounted by several divisions of Viet Minh. Cogny's notion, although there is no independent evidence that Navarre was aware of it, was to secure the mooring point by far-ranging patrol activity which would keep small groups of Viet Minh away from the valley through mobile defence beginning up to fifty miles away.

On 17 July 1953, Navarre presented his plans to the French Joint Chiefs of Staff in Paris, who approved them with the *caveat* that not all the additional supplies and men which Navarre wanted would be available. At the subsequent meeting of the National Defence Committee, Navarre informed the members of the highest policy-forming body in the French defence machinery of his intentions. The Government under Joseph Laniel had decided that the quest for a victory in Indo China would consume more resources than it was worth. Laniel was looking for some means of stabilizing the situation as a preliminary to peace negotiations on the Korean model. In particular, he did not wish Navarre to take grave risks over the preservation of Laotian security. However, these views could not have been made sufficiently clear to Navarre, for one of his major pre-occupations in the coming months was the preparation of plans to keep Giap out of Laos. In reply to Laniel's allegations in his memoirs that Navarre had been instructed to abandon Laos if necessary, Navarre has written that no firm decision was taken on the matter.[14] Furthermore, General Catroux, leader of the Commission of Investigation into the Dien Bien Phu disaster found in 1955 that the first expression of the Government's policy regarding the defence of Laos to Navarre was contained in a directive dated 13 November 1953, and that this directive was not handed to Navarre until 4 December, a fortnight after the first battalions had dropped into Dien Bien Phu.

[14]Henri Navarre, *Agonie de l'Indochine* (Plon, Paris, 1956), p. 338

Consequently, Navarre returned to Saigon feeling that his plans had been fundamentally approved and that some importance was to be attached to Laos. However, while these discussions had been taking place, the first fruits of Navarre's period of office had appeared. In a brilliant and daring raid on the Viet Minh store dumps at Lang Son, French paratroopers had surprised their enemy and destroyed over 5,000 tons of equipment, arms, ammunition and fuel which was being held in storage before being sent to the front. The raiders made their way south-east to the coast in two days, and were picked up and brought back to Hanoi at the cost of very few casualties.

During the first half of August 1953, the garrison of Na San was brought back by air to Hanoi. This difficult manoeuvre was at least partly achieved in the face of the Viet Minh by means of a trick. The commander of Na San broadcast a request for additional battalions in the hope that the Viet Minh radio intercept service would also receive the message. Large numbers of aircraft appeared over Na San, the first few of which dropped more paratroops into the camp so that it would appear to the Viet Minh that the aircraft which were landing on the airstrip were taking troops in, rather than bringing them out. No Viet Minh attack was mounted and the last plane load of French troops escaped without incident. It has also been alleged by Jules Roy that reports of Viet Minh observers of the withdrawal did not get back to Giap because of a radio break-down. It is significant also that Giap has offered another explanation for the French success:

One of our strategic principles consists of trying to retain the initiative at all times. Navarre talked a lot about keeping his. There were not very many troops stationed at Na San, and the time did not coincide with that of our major operations. We considered that if Navarre evacuated the garrison from Na San, well, that suited us fine.[15]

[15]Interview with Jules Roy, cited in Jules Roy, *The Battle of Dien Bien Phu* (Faber & Faber, London; Harper & Row, New York, 1965), p. 22

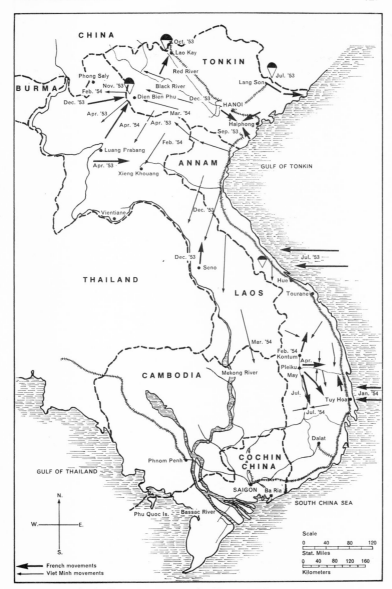

Giap's Countermoves to the Navarre Plan, 1953-54

The patent falsehood of the notion that 'not very many troops' were within Na San indicates that this explanation of Giap's cannot be taken at face value. In the absence of a more plausible reason, it appears that Navarre was able to catch Giap off balance and through good luck and management save the lives of some 10,000 Frenchmen who would otherwise have been in grave danger once the rains had stopped.

The importance of Laos in Navarre's mind was further enhanced when he heard of the signing of the Matignon Agreement between France and Laos on 22 October 1953. This agreement provided for the independence of Laos and for its adherence to the French Union. It was particularly import-ant because Laos was the first of the three Associated States of Indo China to make such an agreement to abide within the French Union. It seemed obvious to Navarre that the main benefit which Laos would derive from the agreement was French protection against the Viet Minh. After the events of early 1953, it appeared certain that Giap would try to thrust deeper into Laos in the coming dry season, and so Navarre felt himself to be under considerable pressure to take counter measures. The intentions of the French Government regard-ing this agreement have not been made clear, but in view of the directive which Navarre received on 4 December 1953, it seems that the official French attitude was to treat it merely as another scrap of paper.

While Navarre had been in Paris in July, his staff in Saigon had issued Directive No. 563, the first document embodying Navarre's plan for a re-occupation of Dien Bien Phu. The new emphasis which the Matignon Agreement had placed on Laotian security forced Navarre to take a major decision—if he were to defend Laos, then the place from which he could best achieve this was Dien Bien Phu. However the location was not sufficient basis for an operational plan. Could the number of troops which Navarre could afford and maintain withstand the number which Giap could send to Dien Bien Phu and supply? French intelligence estimates stated that the Viet Minh could employ one, possibly two, lightly equipped and supported divisions in operations in the Dien Bien Phu area. Navarre could send the greater part of one division into the valley. Experience at Na San had proved that one French division could hold off two Viet Minh divisions operating closer to their sources of supplies than they would be at Dien Bien Phu. Consequently, it looked reasonable to Navarre to go ahead and plan the defence of Laos through the seizure of the most important piece of land near the Laotian border.

On 2 November 1953, Colonel Berteil issued Navarre's Operational Directive No. 852 which nominated Cogny as the commander of an operation to re-occupy Dien Bien Phu at some date preferably between 15 and 20 November and not later than 1 December 1953 with a force of six battalions of paratroops. This concept had no appeal for the commander of Tonkin however, and he replied to Navarre two days later, stressing that occupation of the Dien Bien Phu valley could make little difference to the outcome of the war because the Viet Minh could easily by-pass the French position and walk unopposed into Laos at some other sector. Moreover, Cogny felt that the rice resources of the valley were too meagre to be of great assistance to the Viet Minh, while the numbers of troops whom Giap could send to Dien Bien Phu were sufficiently great to remove any possibility of putting the mooring point notion into practice. Instead, the garrison would be confined within a small perimeter under conditions of siege in which no offensive operations could be mounted against the Viet Minh. Cogny also felt very anxious about the security of the Red River delta, fearing that unless an offensive was mounted there in the near future, the main French support base in Tonkin would collapse. With six of his battalions at Dien Bien Phu, such an offensive would be impossible.

While these objections of Cogny were powerful and, as events turned out, prophetic, they ignored one important factor. The siege of Na San had tied down sufficient numbers of Giap's main force and consumed enough of his supplies to force a crippling delay on the drive into Laos. It was a long way from the Viet Bac to the Mekong valley and any sizeable check en route could prevent the Viet Minh from reaching their goals before the next rainy season broke. Unless Giap cared to establish a major forward base close to the Laotian border and vulnerable to French attack, he had to have an almost uninterrupted passage through to the Mekong in order to conquer sufficient of Laos to avoid a complete withdrawal during the coming monsoon rains. Therefore, despite further letters of protest from Cogny, Navarre felt justified in ordering preparations for *Operation Castor*, the seizure of the valley by paratroops, to continue. Cogny did not feel sufficiently sure of his ground to press the matter further and so the slide into disaster began.

Navarre also received objections to *Operation Castor* from Colonel Nicot, the officer commanding the air transport of the French forces in Indo China. Nicot stated, in writing, that his aircraft were incapable of maintaining a constant flow of supplies to Dien Bien Phu in view of the poor weather conditions which prevailed over the valley, the ease with which Viet Minh anti-aircraft batteries could be set up around the rim of the valley, and the state of repair of his aircraft. Nicot's protests were supported by Brigadier General Deschaux, commander of the French Air Force in Tonkin. He stressed that the huge distances involved in supporting Dien Bien Phu from Hanoi, two hundred miles each way, would reduce the effectiveness of his aircraft over Dien Bien Phu to a few minutes each while the cost in fuel, crew time and engine wear would be enormous. Navarre did not waver in front of these objections which, he held, could be overcome with determination on the part of those involved in the supply system.

Cogny had selected Brigadier General Gilles to lead the assault into the valley, and he instructed him on 11 and 12 November that the nature of the operation was merely to secure his mooring point. In particular, the defence of the Dien Bien Phu airstrip would 'exclude any system designed to provide a belt of strongpoints for the airfield'.[16] The date of

[16]Bernard Fall, *op. cit.*, p. 37

the operation was set for 20 November and the final stages of planning began.

By happy coincidence, the new Minister for the Associated States, Marc Jacquet, former Mayor of Barbizon, had arrived by air in Saigon on 15 November. Navarre took him, together with High Commissioner Dejean and Vietnamese Prime Minister Nguyen Van Tam, to Hanoi for a briefing on *Operation Castor*. Jacquet was apparently unaware of the vital instruction of the National Defence Council requesting modification of Navarre's plans. This had been sent to his office in Paris while he had been flying to Saigon. He did not see anything in *Operation Castor* which urgently required that the French Government be informed, so presumably even he was unaware of the policy that nothing was to be risked for the sake of Laos. His staff in Paris did not bother to forward the instruction by express means but after a few days sent an envoy, Admiral Cabanier, to pass the content of the instruction directly to Navarre.

As fate would have it, Cabanier arrived in Saigon on 19 November after Navarre had departed for Hanoi. Cabanier telephoned Navarre to announce his intention of coming up to Hanoi as soon as possible. Navarre told him to wait in Saigon until he returned late that day, and to call on him on the morning of 20 November. Navarre may have suspected that Cabanier was bringing some instruction which would spoil months of his work and planning, while the presentation of a *fait accompli* would take him beyond the reach of the new directive. Thus the paratroops dropped into Dien Bien Phu several hours before the first intimations of the Government's Laotian policy were made clear to Navarre.

When Navarre received Cabanier's message that he was to reconsider his plans, he showed Cabanier the operation order for *Castor*. This was Navarre's answer to the National Defence Council's invitation to reconsider his plans. Success in halting the Viet Minh thrust into Laos, rather than complacent toleration of Giap's coming offensive, would place France in a much better position for bargaining around a conference table about a peace settlement. However, the confidence with which Navarre had rejected the suggestions of the National Defence Council increased, as Navarre ought to have realized, the already appreciable risks which he was accepting at Dien Bien Phu. If he got into trouble, he knew that he could appeal to the French Government for assistance only at the cost of his reputation—perhaps, at that point, the dearest thing in life to Navarre.

He had committed several thousand men to a remote although important area against the wishes of the man who had to command the whole operation and of those who had to fly in the supplies on which the life of the garrison depended. The paratroops in the valley had been ordered to construct only light formal defences and not to get involved in a siege which they were poorly equipped to handle, yet which would be forced on them if Giap reacted in sufficient strength to make the mounting of *Operation Castor* worthwhile from the French point of view. If the situation looked like deteriorating, Navarre was well aware that he could expect little assistance beyond the resources under his command which were already over-stretched to cover their commitments.

Why had Navarre chosen to put so many of the best men of his force in jeopardy, thereby risking the stability of the entire French position in Indo China? The answer depends on three factors. He believed while he was planning the operation that the French Government felt it important for him to defend Laos, and that the signing of the Matignon Agreement confirmed this policy. If Laos were to be defended, then the strategic—as distinct from the tactical—characteristics of the Dien Bien Phu valley made this a logical point from which to conduct this defence. Finally the intelligence estimates that Giap could concentrate one or possibly two of his divisions at Dien Bien Phu and support them with only meagre quantities of artillery indicated that the force at Navarre's disposal for Dien Bien Phu, approximately one division, could both provide for its own protection and cause sufficient inconvenience to the Viet Minh to frustrate their drive into Laos. It has already been seen that Navarre was mistaken in his concept of French Government policy, yet the Government did not repudiate his actions. The words and deeds of his enemy, Vo Nguyen Giap, have confirmed his view of the strategic importance of Dien Bien Phu. It now remains to examine the quality of the vital intelligence estimates whose correctness or otherwise held the fate of *Operation Castor* in the balance.

8 Dien Bien Phu — The Battle

While Navarre and his colleagues had been making these elaborate and ambitious plans, Giap and the Viet Minh High Command had been taking stock of their own situation. At the end of the 1952/53 campaign season, Giap's forces were scattered over Tonkin and northern Laos, remote from their main bases, short of supplies and exhausted after months of fighting across over 100 miles of jungle and mountain country. It had certainly been a successful campaign, in which the French had been forced out of western Tonkin and northern Laos, but Giap now had to plan his reaction to a possible French attempt to regain some of this country, while at the same time avoid being drawn into a major action which would divert his own strategy from its course.

The French pacification offensive in the Red River delta during the wet season characterized the problem which confronted Giap. As he has written, the problem was:

> The enemy was concentrating forces in the Red River delta, and launching attacks on our free zones. Now, had we to concentrate our forces to face the enemy, or to mobilize them for attacks in other directions? The problem was difficult. In concentrating our forces to fight the enemy in the delta, we could extend our free zone; but here [i.e. in the delta] the enemy was still strong and we could easily be decimated. On the other hand, in attacking in other directions with our main forces, we could exploit the

vulnerable points of the enemy to annihilate the bulk of their forces; but our free zone would thus be threatened.[17]

It was unfortunate for the French that Navarre did not see the vulnerability of the Viet Minh held territory close to the delta. Giap decided to take a chance on the security of his rear areas in order to force the French out into the more remote areas where they were at a disadvantage.

Giap's insight into the dilemma facing Navarre in 1953 is shown in his writings on the strategic direction of his campaign for 1953/4:

> The enemy found himself face to face with a contradiction: without scattering his forces it was impossible for him to occupy the invaded territory; in scattering his forces, he put himself in difficulties. His scattered units would fall easy prey to our troops, his mobile forces would be more and more reduced and the shortage of troops would be all the more acute. On the other hand if he concentrated his forces to move from the defensive position and cope with us with more initiative, the occupation forces would be weakened and it would be difficult for him to hold the invaded territory. Now, if the enemy gives up occupied territory, the very aim of the war of re-conquest is defeated.[18]

We have seen the answer Navarre gave to these problems in the plan announced to his regional commanders in Saigon on 16 June 1953. In trying to cope with both points of the dilemma, he had left himself vulnerable to both because he simply did not have sufficient strength to hold the areas he had and to concentrate a special force for mounting an offensive. Giap correctly read Navarre's intention to oppose a Viet Minh thrust into Laos by a forward defence, and so he set about creating a number of widely scattered threats to French posts so that as soon as Navarre had gathered together a number of battalions in one area he would have to disperse some of them to rescue a remote outpost before he could proceed with his major offensive. Giap continued this series of diversionary

[17]Giap, *op. cit.*, p. 198
[18]Giap, *op. cit.*, p. 159

operations for so long that Navarre was forced to launch the assault on Dien Bien Phu with far fewer reserves than he had intended.*

In the Red River delta, the Viet Minh regulars and guerrillas were ordered to engage in an outbreak of harassing actions, ambushes, sniping, assassination of Bao Dai's officials, and raids on small sentry posts along the de Lattre line. Route 5 between Hanoi and Haiphong was continually cut, and several French battalions had to be stationed in its vicinity to keep it open for supply convoys.

Viet Minh activity in central Laos was stepped up to create a major threat to Thakhek and Seno, the main French air base in the region. Joint action with the Pathet Lao forced the French out of Thakhek and more battalions had to be flown into Seno from the Red River delta and the Saigon area. The defence of Seno was successful, but it tied down more of Navarre's troops just after he had committed his first battalions to Dien Bien Phu. Moving around Seno, the Viet Minh attacked and entered Attopeu, and achieved effective control over the Bolovens Plateau, the important strategic highland of Southern Laos. From this position, the flank of the French in the Central Highlands of Vietnam could be turned.

Operation Atlante went ashore on the southern coast of Annam in January 1954, and so Giap ordered the main Viet Minh forces in the area, two independent regiments, to withdraw, leaving only rearguard elements to harass the French, while a new wave of attacks was made on the western part of the Central Highlands, taking first Dak To, north west of Kontum, then Kon Brai, north east of Kontum, and then Kontum itself. From this major town of the Highlands, Viet Minh control spread gradually southwards to Route 19, the only link between the other two important towns of the Central Highlands, Pleiku and An Khe. More French reinforcements had to be scraped up to keep these centres from falling.

In February 1954, Giap launched another offensive into northern Laos, aimed at Phong Saly and, indirectly, at Luang

*For the locations of these offensives described below see map p. 127.

Prabang. The French reacted as Giap wished and stretched themselves yet further to reinforce the Royal Laotian capital. The Viet Minh raids also forced the French to disperse troops being concentrated near Muong Khoua in north-eastern Laos in order to relieve the pressure on the Dien Bien Phu garrison.

Through these four diversionary actions, Giap had forced Navarre to concentrate forces at five points sufficiently far apart to prevent any of these concentrations supporting one another. It was a warning to Navarre that he lacked the strength to both hold his present position and engage in a major battle for any length of time. It was doubly clever of Giap to exert himself and his regiments so vigorously, for not only did these moves tie down French reserves, but they led the French High Command to believe that whatever Giap could do at Dien Bien Phu, it would be on a small scale, since he had committed so much of his supposedly slender resources elsewhere.

While Giap had been planning these moves in the latter part of 1953, international events began to impinge on the Viet Minh leaders to give the attainment of their goals an added degree of urgency. The acceleration of the tempo of the Cold War in the early 1950s had given both the world power blocs a stake in the outcome of the Indo China war. However, the stalemate which seemed to have developed—in which the French could not be ejected from the major centres of population and the Viet Minh had an unbreakable hold over the Vietnamese nationalist movement—threatened to precipitate another confrontation on the Korean model, which neither the Russians nor the Americans wanted. Britain and China were similarly inclined, and so there were powerful diplomatic forces at the disposal of a mutual desire for peace. The French government had begun to despair of a military solution in early 1953—they had even gone so far as to instruct General Salan on 24 April to accept territorial losses rather than to undertake operations which might endanger the security of the Expeditionary Corps. The content of this directive seems to have been ignored by all concerned in the planning of late

1953—Navarre has claimed that Salan did not even bring it to his notice.

The world was surprised on 29 November 1953 to read in the Swedish newspaper *Expressen* that the Viet Minh were also ready to commence negotiations. In a series of answers to questions submitted by journalist Sven Löfgen, Ho Chi Minh stated:

> If the French Government, after having absorbed the lessons of these war years, desires to conclude an armistice and resolve the question of Vietnam by negotiations, the people and the government of the Democratic Republic of Vietnam are ready to examine the French proposals. . . . The basis for an armistice is that the French Government really respects Vietnam's independence. . . . The negotiation of an armistice concerns essentially the government of France and that of Vietnam.[19]

It had been thought by most observers that if anyone had anything to gain by a continuation of the war, it was the Viet Minh. However, Ho had succumbed either to joint Sino-Soviet pressure or to fear of American assistance to the French, and thus the last barrier to negotiations had been overcome. Two days before the publication of Ho's statements and therefore probably several days after he had made them since they had to be transmitted through Peking, the Soviet accepted Western proposals for a meeting of the Big Four (Britain, France, the Soviet Union and the United States) to discuss European problems on the proviso that she would raise the question of a five power conference, including China, to settle the main problems of Asia. The four power conference met in Berlin on 25 January 1954 and agreed that a five power conference should meet in Geneva in April to settle the Korean and Indo Chinese problems.

The important factor for Giap's consideration was that from late November, he knew that he could not count on being able to use his military strength against the French after April or

---

[19]J. Lacouture and P. Devillers: *La Fin d'une Guerre: Indochine 1954* (Editions du Seuil, Paris, 1960), p. 45; *End of a War: Geneva, 1954* (Frederick A. Praeger, New York, 1969).

May of the following year. Consequently, he had a great incentive to strike hard at any possible target which the French exposed. Once he had realized how anxious the French government were for a settlement, he was also in a position to take a small gamble on the state of his forces after May 1954. Therefore it did not matter as much as in earlier years if he became locked in a desperate and bloody battle between November and May at the cost of considerable casualties to his own divisions, provided that he could thereby inflict equal damage to the French.

These were some of the thoughts which must have been in Giap's mind when he received the news that the French had landed several battalions of troops at Dien Bien Phu on 20 November. He states that the first problem he had to resolve was whether to place a small force around the French to contain the garrison while his main force was left free for mobile operations, or whether to make a direct attack with the bulk of his main force on the Dien Bien Phu garrison and leave the diversionary offensives to local forces.[20] Dien Bien Phu was obviously the main feature of the French strategy for the coming months and so they had much to lose by a defeat there.

> However, the importance of Dien Bien Phu could not be regarded as a decisive factor in our decision to attack it. In the relation of forces at that time, could we destroy the fortified entrenched camp of Dien Bien Phu? Could we be certain of victory in attacking it? Our decision had to depend on this consideration alone.
>
> Dien Bien Phu was a very strongly fortified entrenched camp. But on the other hand, it was set up in a mountainous region, on ground which was advantageous to us, and decidedly disadvantageous to the enemy. Dien Bien Phu was, moreover, a completely isolated position, far away from all the enemy's bases. The only means of supplying Dien Bien Phu was by air. These circumstances could easily deprive the enemy of all initiative and force him on to the defensive if attacked.
>
> On our side, we had picked units of the regular army which we could concentrate to achieve supremacy in power. We could

[20]Giap's appreciation of the situation at Dien Bien Phu is given in *People's War People's Army, op. cit.,* pp. 166-9

overcome all difficulties in solving the necessary tactical problems; we had, in addition, an immense rear, and the problem of
supplying the front with food and ammunition, though very
difficult, was not insoluble. Thus we had conditions for retaining
the initiative in the operations.

It was on the basis of this analysis of the enemy's and our own
strong and weak points that we solved the question as to whether
we should attack Dien Bien Phu or not. *We decided to wipe out
at all costs the whole enemy force at Dien Bien Phu,* [Giap's
italics] after having created favourable conditions for this battle
by launching numerous offensives on various battlefields and by
intensifying preparations on the Dien Bien Phu battlefield.

This classic of clear military thought and expression shows
how soundly reasoned were Giap's plans. Without bogging
himself down in the detailed tactical points relating to a battle
at Dien Bien Phu, Giap's mind was able to select the crucially
important strategic factors, deduce that he had sufficient
strength to undertake the operation and to outline the fundamental concept of the development of the battle, viz. disper-

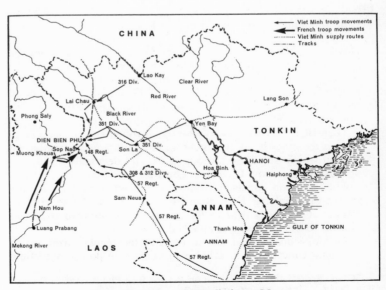

Dien Bien Phu—the Preliminary Moves

sion of French efforts through many other offensives, while
he made lengthy and gradual preparations for an assault on
Dien Bien Phu aimed at killing every Frenchman in the garrison, even at the cost of heavy casualties to his own men.

As soon as he had decided upon his plan, Giap set his divisions in motion. 316 Division, the closest to Dien Bien Phu,
was ordered to threaten Lai Chau and to annihilate French
units moving from there to Dien Bien Phu. 148 Regiment
which was in the valley when the French paratroops were
dropped was given a watching and harassing role on the out-
skirts of the French positions. 308, 312 and 351 (Heavy)
Divisions were ordered to leave their bases in the area of Phu
Tho - Yen Bay - Thai Nguyen in late November, cross the
Red River by ferries at the rate of 6,000 per night from 3
December, and then move to prepared underwater bridges
across the Black River on their way to Dien Bien Phu. 304
Division which was near Thanh Hoa, south of the Red River
delta, was ordered to provide one regiment, and in early
December it dispatched the 57th on its 250-mile march to
Dien Bien Phu. Moving at the rate of from fifteen to twenty
miles per day, the thirty-three battalions of infantry, six regiments of artillery and one regiment of engineers which made
up Giap's force were closing in on Navarre's six battalions of
infantry, one regiment of artillery and single company of
engineers. By Christmas 1953, the intelligence estimates on
which the whole of Navarre's gamble had rested had been
proved wrong by a factor of three, and the outcome of the
battle was taken out of the realm of guessing.

Navarre's concept of the role of the Dien Bien Phu garrison
had been hardening throughout late November. The mooring
point idea was given away completely in favour of a fortified
camp from which a pitched defensive battle could be fought.
This notion was passed on to Cogny in a directive of 3 December 1953 which included Navarre's (or his staff's) forecast of
the timetable of the battle: several weeks would elapse while
the Viet Minh were moving their forces into position, then
would come a reconnaissance phase of from six to ten days

and finally the assault which would last several days, 'and
which must end with the failure of the Viet Minh offensive.'[21]
This estimate was as far from reality as that of the Viet Minh
strength. Although the movement phase occupied only six
weeks, the reconnaissance took nearly one hundred days and
the battle continued at a furious pace for fifty-six days.

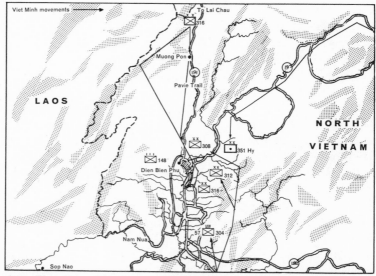

Dien Bien Phu—Giap Concentrates his Forces, November 1953—January
1954

French intelligence had intercepted some of Giap's orders to
his divisions, and by 28 November, Navarre must have been
aware that the whole basis of his plan to defend Dien Bien Phu
was crumbling. Nonetheless he ordered *Operation Atlante* to
go ahead in the South and reinforced Dien Bien Phu by only
another four battalions of infantry and four batteries of artillery. However, he saw at least the theoretical possibility of a
forced withdrawal under overwhelming Viet Minh pressure
and began to consider plans to meet such a crisis. In Directive

[21]IPS 949/EMIFT/3/TS issued by General Navarre, 3 December 1953,
cited in Fall, *op. cit.*, p. 49

No. 178 of 29 December 1953, he ordered Cogny to prepare a detailed withdrawal plan. Cogny's answer of 21 January 1954 was accompanied by the reservation that the prospects of a successful withdrawal in the face of such Viet Minh superiority were so dismal that the garrison would be better advised to stay within their defences and fight it out, no matter what losses they suffered. To try to fight a path through the enemy girdle of four times the French numbers, after the Viet Minh had been able to dig in and prepare themselves to meet such an eventuality, would be suicide according to Navarre's chief subordinate.

Cogny was quite right in adding this reservation. Once the first divisions of Giap's main force had reached Dien Bien Phu the trap was closed. This was a vastly different case to that of Na San. The Viet Minh on the hilltops could see everything going on in the valley and an attempt to fly troops out or to leave on foot would be noticed at once. The first one or two battalions might escape by air, but the fate of the diminished remainder would be a predictable catastrophe. After the first fortnight of December 1953, the men of the Dien Bien Phu garrison could hope only for strength to endure everything that the Viet Minh could hurl against them if they were to survive the coming weeks and months.

But what grounds were there for these hopes? Caught at a severe strategic disadvantage, the French troops were dependent entirely on tactical superiority for their security. Did the tactical situation confer advantages on the French sufficient to offset their strategic disadvantages?

The most striking feature of the tactical dispositions of the opposing forces was that the Viet Minh were up on the hillsides, overlooking and dominating the French who were down in the valley. One French theory justifying a battle under these conditions was that since the crest of the hill line was so far away, the Viet Minh would have to expose themselves on the forward slopes of these hills, where the French could see both them and any artillery pieces which they attempted to use. In practice, this theory proved particularly empty. The hills were

too far away for close French observation from the ground
and they were covered with jungle thick enough to conceal a
large amount of activity even from close air reconnaissance.
The forward slopes of the surrounding hills did not present a
perfectly smooth face to the valley, and in the wrinkles and
folds created by secondary hills at lower levels than the main
crest line, the Viet Minh were entirely protected from the
eyes of the men in the valley.

French maps showed the floor of the valley as a flat expanse
of open paddy fields, with no refuge or cover for anyone
foolish enough to launch an attack across them. It therefore
looked well suited to the employment of tanks, and a squadron
was provided. These conditions probably had a lot to do with
the choice of a cavalryman, Colonel Christian de Castries,
as commander of the garrison. However, much of the valley
floor was covered by thick bush, much higher than it looked
from the air, in which tanks were of small use, while an attacking force could conceal itself at several points, safe from discovery by all means except a French patrol.

The initial differences between the concepts of Navarre and
Cogny regarding the defence of the valley resulted in only
lightly equipped troops being committed to a defence which
required the heaviest support available. The replacement of
some paratroop battalions by infantry was of assistance, but it
did not make up for the loss of time occasioned when the first
paratroops neglected to commence digging massive defences.
So much patrolling effort was called for to keep the Viet Minh
away from the French defences in the first weeks of 1954 that
progress on the defences was severely retarded.

The need to be able to deliver massive amounts of artillery
fire onto the ground immediately in front of the airfield defences led the French to split their garrison into two parts. One
third of their strength was stationed in an outpost called
Isabelle, a few miles to the south of the main position. While
the basic idea behind this split was sound, *Isabelle* was sited
too far to the south to be able to give fire support to the two
northern outposts, *Gabrielle* and *Beatrice*. Thus the Viet Minh

in attacking these two outposts had to contend with only two thirds of the moderate French artillery strength. In order to protect the guns at *Isabelle*, it was necessary to tie down over two battalions of infantry, or 1,400 combat troops out of a total of 5,300.

The way in which the French artillery was employed casts grave doubts on the capability of the French gunnery officers involved. To face Giap's six regiments of field artillery, which included 105 mm. howitzers, an equal match for the French, Cogny allocated approximately one quarter of this strength. Never believing that the Viet Minh had 105 mm. weapons and the capacity to supply them at a high rate with ammunition, the French counter-bombardment capacity was a meagre four 155 mm. guns. In the face of the firepower opposing them, they might just as well have not had these guns. Strange to relate, this shortage of artillery was not something which had been forced on the garrison commander by Hanoi or Saigon— there were new American weapons still in their crates in Haiphong ample to have trebled the Dien Bien Phu strength. But in the light of the intelligence estimates provided, the artillery commander at Dien Bien Phu, Colonel Piroth, assured his superiors that he would be able to silence any artillery which the Viet Minh were rash enough to use within minutes of their opening fire.

Not only could the positioning of the French artillery be criticized for taking fire support away from the northern outposts, but the actual emplacements of the individual guns left a great deal to be desired. Being in the centre of a valley, the guns had to be able to traverse in any direction. The construction of overhead protection for the guns to meet this requirement is not easy, but it is nonetheless possible. However, contemptuous of Giap's firepower, Piroth felt that such efforts were unnecessary and so the guns were merely placed in open circular pits with no overhead protection. Once the battle began in earnest, Piroth's gunners had great difficulty in firing their weapons, and many of the guns themselves were damaged by the Viet Minh bombardments. It is little wonder that Piroth committed suicide soon after the battle commenced.

The construction of defensive positions which have to stand up to artillery bombardment calls for materials of great strength—rock or deep diggings in well compacted earth, steel supports, concrete, stout timber baulks, sheet iron, and sandbags in enormous quantities. However, the shortage of French airlift capacity reduced the quantity of defence materials which could be flown in to one tenth of the estimated requirements. The natural resources of Dien Bien Phu could provide very little to substitute for the remaining nine tenths. There was little suitable structural timber, and the local soil, a fine alluvial powder, lost its cohesion when bombarded so that bunkers collapsed leaving their inmates standing in a heap of fine dust from which it was impossible to reconstruct the fortifications.

Flooding of the defences during the monsoon rains was also an acute problem which was never overcome. French engineers mapped the areas subject to inundation but the lack of time and materials defeated plans to re-site the position. When particularly heavy rains began in April 1954, most strongpoints were partly flooded and the *Isabelle* defenders found themselves floundering in a swamp. The flooding also weakened the structural strength of the trenches so that even if they did escape the effects of the Viet Minh artillery, many parts of the defences simply caved in and defied attempts to rebuild them with the pathetically inadequate materials available.

The senior officers of the French Air Force had already warned Navarre that it would be very doubtful whether they could fly in the huge amount of supplies required to support 10,000 men in a major battle. Daily re-supply needs amounted to over 150 tons, and assuming perfect conditions for delivery, the aircraft could just deliver this quantity. However, these figures made no provision for initial establishment needs such as the steel plates for the air strip and so the system got behind right from the start. When the actual air conditions over Dien

Bien Phu are examined it becomes apparent that they were far from perfect for delivery. The weather was often so bad that no aircraft could land and parachutes could not be dropped over the French positions with accuracy. The approach lines for aircraft landing, taking off, or dropping parachutes permitted very little manoeuvre, and rendered the French and American aircraft delivering the supplies highly vulnerable to Giap's anti-aircraft batteries, which were clustered around the narrow head of the valley. Consequently, the slender resources of the French Air Force were steadily reduced by losses over Dien Bien Phu and the supply problem for the defenders grew more and more acute. When the day came that French aircraft could no longer land on the air strip because of Viet Minh artillery, maximum delivery rates declined to some ninety tons per day. The ammunition consumption of the defenders had to be reduced accordingly, and the last weeks of the battle were fought by many men on half rations.

This then was the tactical predicament of the French garrison—instead of offering a counterweight to Giap's strategic superiority, it made the future so hopeless for the French troops that it is amazing that their discipline held once the soldiers had perceived the nature of their disadvantages.

However, Viet Minh success cannot be taken for granted simply because the French were fighting under a number of difficulties. Not only did the Viet Minh have their own problems, but events showed that the French were capable of fighting sufficiently hard to withstand a colossal pounding for fifty-six days during which they killed several thousand of their attackers. In order to win the battle, Giap had to make a number of important decisions, which, had they been poor, could have raised his casualty level and consumption of supplies sufficiently to leave the outcome a stalemate. This result at the time of the Geneva conference would have been most harmful to Viet Minh standing throughout the world and could have led to a hardening of popular attitudes in France for an additional period of war.

Once Giap had decided that he would fight a major battle

at Dien Bien Phu, he asked himself 'how should we do it?'[22]
Should he attempt to carry the position by a rapid assault
before the French had sufficient time to consolidate their defences, or should he fight a long and inevitably costly battle of
attrition in which the vulnerability of the French supply
system would swing the verdict in Giap's favour? Giap saw the
problem thus:

> By concentrating superior forces, we could push simultaneously
> from many directions deep into enemy positions, cut the fortified
> entrenched camp into many separate parts, then swiftly annihi-
> late the entire enemy manpower. There were many obvious
> advantages if we could strike swiftly to win swiftly: by launching
> a big offensive with fresh troops, we could shorten the duration of
> the campaign and avoid the wear and tear of a long operation.
> As the campaign would not last long, the supplying of the
> battlefront could be ensured without difficulty. However, on
> further examining the question, we saw that these tactics had a
> very great, a basic disadvantage: our troops lacked experience in
> attacking fortified entrenched camps. If we wanted to win swiftly,
> success could not be ensured. For that reason, in the process of
> making preparations, we continued to follow the enemy's situa-
> tion and checked and re-checked our potentialities again. And
> we came to the conclusion that we could not secure success if
> we struck swiftly. In consequence, *we resolutely chose the other
> tactic: to strike surely and advance surely.* In taking this correct
> decision, *we strictly followed this fundamental principle of the
> conduct of a revolutionary war: strike to win, strike only when
> success is certain; if it is not, then don't strike.*[23]

This reasoning throws interesting light on Giap's growing
conservatism in strategic and tactical matters, showing that the
rash attacker of Vinh Yen, Mao Khe, the Day River line and
Na San had learned from his mistakes. The emphasis he gives
to checking and re-checking his strength relative to the French
indicates that this decision was far from easy for him to make.
Apart from what may be assumed from his earlier battles to
be a natural desire for quick results, Giap was also under pres-

---

[22]Giap, *op. cit.*, p. 169. This discussion of Giap's tactical control of the
battle is based on his account in *People's War People's Army*, pp. 169-217
[23]Giap, *op. cit.*, pp. 169-170. The italics are Giap's.

sure to produce a victory before the Geneva conference had
settled the future of Vietnam. Therefore, while his plan may
be criticized for its lack of inspiration in descending to that
lowest of the tactics, attrition, he must have felt that this was
the only feasible solution.

In saying that his troops were inexperienced in attacking
fortified entrenched camps however, he was stating something
less than the truth, for each of his divisions at Dien Bien Phu
had participated in the attacks on the de Lattre line and most
had been engaged in similar battles in the Tonkinese highlands
around Tu Le, Nghia Lo, Na San and Muong Khoua. Had he
said that his troops had not shown that they could master such
defences without elaborate preparations, he would have been
closer to the truth.

Once he had decided on a protracted battle, he had a number of specific problems to overcome: the supply problem for
several months of sustained activity, the difficulties of fighting
in the monsoon rains due in April and the doubts amongst his
own soldiers as to whether the added hardships of a long struggle were worth the effort which they would have to make.

> . . . not everybody was immediately convinced of the correctness
> of these tactics. We patiently educated our men, pointed out that
> there were real difficulties, but that our task was to overcome
> them to create good conditions for the great victory which we
> sought.[24]

Giap evidently had to face a real test of leadership in persuading his men that his method was the most efficient. While
the Communist system of political supervision at all levels gave
Giap a much firmer control over his troops than in a Western
army, he did not treat his men like mindless automatons but
explained to them the reasons for his difficult choice. However,
because the Communist system did enable him to suppress
minor rumblings amongst his men, it is evident that the opposition to the notion of a lengthy battle at Dien Bien Phu was
significant within Viet Minh ranks.

[24]Giap, *op. cit.*, pp. 170-1

The organization of his supply system was a major triumph for Giap and a tribute to the devotion with which hundreds of thousands served the cause. Roads were built across the wildest country, nearly 1,000 trucks were engaged in delivering his supplies, supported by a multitude of porters and men who pushed thousands of bicycles, each laden with some two hundred pounds. The French made efforts to disrupt these transport agencies by bombing, but as has been shown in the mid 1960s, huge amounts of air power can be very ineffective against jungle supply lines. Chinese and Soviet support for the Viet Minh reached new heights while local food resources were tapped throughout the whole of Tonkin and the northern region of Annam. Once again, French estimates of Viet Minh capability were shown to be far short of reality.

While the supply build up was progressing throughout January and February 1954, Giap had to turn his mind to more specific problems connected with the tactics of the coming battle. His intention during the supply phase was to confine the French within a small area of fortifications by aggressive patrolling around the garrison perimeter. During this period, he was able to see that the French position, despite its weaknesses, had to be regarded very seriously.

> The enemy's estimates were obviously wishful thinking but they were not totally without foundation. In fact, the Dien Bien Phu fortified entrenched camp had many strong points which had given our army new problems of tactics to solve before we could annihilate the enemy.[25]

Giap was prepared to show his enemy a little more respect than that enemy displayed towards him.

Because of the skill with which the various strong points of the French defences had been sited, with interlocking and mutually supporting fields of fire, Giap decided to overcome them by a method of 'progressive attack'. While bombarding the fire support elements of the garrison, Giap planned to concentrate his infantry on a narrow and changing front to

[25]Giap, *op. cit.*, p. 173

achieve overwhelming local superiority against first one bunker, then another and so on. To minimize the effectiveness of the French artillery, tanks and air force, he ordered the construction of 'a whole network of trenches that encircled and strangled the entrenched camp, thus creating conditions for our men to deploy and move under enemy fire'.[26] These trenches were gradually advanced until they came within a few yards of some of the French defences. Often they were tunnelled, and the French had no idea that the Viet Minh were so close.

Giap also had to install and protect his artillery. The hillsides of Dien Bien Phu were well suited to the methods used by the Chinese in Korea for emplacing their guns securely. Casemates were dug out of the steep slopes in great secrecy, and the guns were dragged at night, inch by inch, into their positions. The casemates were faced with several feet of earth and camouflaged. Only a small hole was left for the gun to fire through, and a special cover was made for this opening which was removed at the time of firing. Giap was careful not to reveal his possession of 105 mm. guns, and therefore very little of the artillery was used until the battle began in March, in order to surprise the French in their insufficiently strengthened bunkers. Giap was able to obtain anti-aircraft guns and crews from the Chinese in order to restrict the flow of French supplies. These were also installed carefully in the areas where they could achieve the greatest effect, with dire consequences for the garrison when the battle was at its height.

Thus, from his forward command post near Tuan Giao, Giap was able to make very effective use of the time necessary for the preparatory phase, without unduly revealing his strength and thereby provoking heavy French air attacks on his assembling forces and supply dumps. With the methods outlined above as the basis for his battle, Giap then decided which of the outposts would be the first to be attacked. The inability of the guns at *Isabelle* to support the two northern outposts made them a desirable target. Furthermore, they were

[26]Giap, *op. cit.*, p. 174. The italics are Giap's

on hilltops which looked directly onto the airfield and the central French position. Once he had them in his hands Giap could prevent any use of the airfield and pour observed fire down into the French positions at any sign of activity. He could then proceed to isolate *Isabelle* from the main defences and start to eat them away, a post at a time, until they had been reduced to a level which could not withstand an all-out assault. Then he could administer the *coup de grâce* and victory would be his.

The first phase began on 13 March with the overwhelming of *Beatrice*, the outpost to the north-east of the airfield. On the following night, *Gabrielle*, the most northerly outpost, fell. In each case, Giap had launched attacks of almost divisional strength against battalion positions, supported with heavy mortar and artillery bombardments which caved in the defences. By 17 March, the Viet Minh had achieved all that Giap had wished for in the first phase, and preparation began for the second.

After a lull in the battle for thirteen days, the second phase began on 30 March. Miles of trenches had been dug by the Viet Minh during their preparations, encircling the airfield defences in a number of concentric rings linked by many radial trenches which approached within grenade throwing distance of the French perimeter. The French made strenuous efforts to prevent strangulation by these excavations, but they simply did not have sufficient air power, artillery and infantry to cause other than nuisance damage to Giap's master plan. Once Giap had launched his Alamein, pressure was maintained at such a level on the French that they were hard put to hold their existing perimeter without taking offensive action against the covered approaches of the Viet Minh.

Giap planned his attack to take place as a number of overlapping waves. Just as the French were fully engaged in holding an assault on one part of the perimeter, another would come into another sector, causing the French to divert their reserves while reserves existed and to weaken their defence of

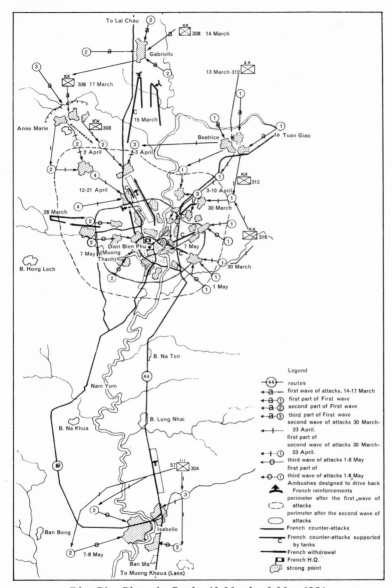

Dien Bien Phu—the Battle, 13 March—8 May 1954

the first threatened area to strengthen the second once reserves
had been consumed. These attacks were no small affairs, for
they were usually made in proportions which gave the Viet
Minh a numerical advantage of from five to one to ten to one,
with a division pitted against a single battalion.

The first attack was made on the eastern sector where the
French had several strong points on five knolls. A French
counter attack forced 312 and 316 Divisions to yield a certain
amount of the perimeter which they had seized but it was not
sufficient to force the Viet Minh off most of the knolls, leaving
them with domination over the heart of the French headquarters and supply areas as well as the airfield which was
never re-opened to French aircraft. While the French counter
attack was under way, 308 Division attacked the northern
sector and drove in towards the end of the air strip. While the
battle was developing around the northern strong points and
the French were desperately making another counter attack,
a new outburst of fighting began on the eastern flank. In this
the French did remarkably well to regain two of the strong
points whose occupation they had been sharing with the Viet
Minh for the past few days.

The weight of the battle swung back to the north on 12
April, with thrusts on the western edge accompanying as part
of 308 Division's assault. Gradually the French were forced
back down the airfield and their area was reduced to a square
a little over a mile across. This complicated the dropping of
supplies. French aircraft had to drop from considerable
heights in order to avoid the anti-aircraft barrage, and so the
parachutes could not be aimed with the necessary precision.
Consequently, much of the ammunition which was meant for
the French went to the Viet Minh, thereby easing Giap's problems at the same time.

The severity of the fighting in April made a heavy impact
on both sides. Giap makes two points which illustrate the
problems he had to cope with to sustain the morale and faith
in victory of his troops.

Each day, thousands of letters and telegrams from all over the country came to the Dien Bien Phu front. Never had Vietnam been so anxious about her fighting sons, never had the relations between the rear and the front been so intimate as in this Winter-Spring campaign.[27]

and

This does not mean that, even when the Dien Bien Phu battle was at its height, negative factors never appeared. *To maintain and develop this determination to fight and to win was a whole process of unremitting and patient political and ideological education and struggle,* tireless and patient efforts in political work on the front line. This was a great achievement of the Party's organizations and branches and of its cadres. After a series of resounding victories, we found in our ranks signs of under-estimation of the enemy. By criticism, we rectified this state of mind in good time. In the long period of preparation, particularly after the second phase of the campaign, when attack and defence were equally fierce, negative rightist thoughts cropped up again to the detriment of the carrying out of the task. In accordance with the instructions of the Political Bureau, we opened in the heart of the battlefield an intensive and extensive struggle against rightist passivity, and for the heightening of revolutionary enthusiasm and the spirit of strict discipline with a view to ensuring the total victory of the campaign. This ideological struggle was very successful.[28]

This confession of the disillusionment within his own ranks is a most revealing statement. Apart from admiring Giap's honesty in publishing it at all, one cannot help wondering what the outcome of the tactical battle at Dien Bien Phu would have been, had Giap not been as much a politician as a soldier. If any Western army had to indulge in massive brainwashing in the midst of a battle in order to maintain discipline and obedience to orders, this would be taken as one of the severest condemnations of its military leadership and of the bankruptcy of its ideological basis.

It is significant that Giap goes on in his next sentence to

[27]Giap, *op. cit.*, p. 184
[28]Giap, *op. cit.*, pp. 180-1. The italics are Giap's

156 GENERAL GIAP

underline the magnitude of the crisis in discipline which he had to face.

> This was one of the greatest achievements in political work in our army's history. It led the Dien Bien Phu campaign to complete victory.[29]

The last days of April were used for a small but much needed respite for Giap's troops, before renewing the attack on the remnants of the French who were running short of food, ammunition, medical supplies, space for burying their dead, and even drinking water, although they were being washed out of their remaining bunkers by monsoon floods. The need for a victory before the Geneva conference began to deal with the Indo China question in detail—it was already in session—drove Giap to renew the attack in early May.

However, though the fighting in April had been desperate and bloody and Viet Minh losses heavier than French, the relative strengths of the two had inclined very much in favour of the Viet Minh. The battles for the outer strong points and the knolls had accomplished the major part of Giap's task. After six days of progressive attacks around the airfield, his three divisions finally overran de Castries' command post on 7 May, and *Isabelle* fell in the early hours of the following morning. The Geneva conference began to discuss Indo China on the afternoon of 8 May.

The goal had been achieved by many factors, several of which were due to Giap. He correctly saw the strategic possibilities of mounting an all-out offensive in early 1954. He appreciated the strengths and weaknesses of the French and of his own forces and adopted a strategy which maximized his own strength and minimized that of his enemy. In fighting the tactical battle he kept within the guidelines of his strategy and never departed from his basic plan for a protracted battle. The problems he encountered were solved by intelligent if unusual means which enabled him to maintain the exertions of his troops sufficiently long to exhaust the French. While no

[29]Giap, *op. cit.*, p. 181

victory would have been possible had his troops not been of high standard and his supply organization copious, neither could it have been achieved without the leadership, organizing ability, tactical and strategic judgement which Giap provided. He had many things helping him but he alone could have ruined the final outcome.

The final act of the Dien Bien Phu drama was acted out at Geneva. The collapse of French desires to continue the war after the psychological impact of their defeat and the reluctance of the United States to take over the burden of the war had guaranteed the Viet Minh control of at least part of Vietnam. The calling of the conference before they had established wider control over the country robbed the Viet Minh of any possibility of avoiding a partition of their country into two, with the northern sector Communist and the southern non-Communist. However, there was the future ahead to take care of that question—at least Ho could be satisfied with half a loaf and legitimacy for the interim.

Despite the conference, Giap did not suspend offensive operations until the actual deadline specified by the armistice —1 August 1954. Even then, some of his units were remarkably slow in acting on the agreement. Lest the French should be inclined to think that the Viet Minh were as exhausted as they were themselves, Giap continued to give them no respite, particularly in the Central Highlands, where most of the French Group Mobile 100, a formation of over three thousand men, was cut to ribbons in a number of brilliantly executed ambushes. Giap also gained control by these actions of several large towns which were in the non-Communist zone, enabling the party cadres to gain a footing before he had to withdraw the bulk of his regular forces to the north of the Ben Hai River which runs through the demilitarized zone designed to keep the two halves of Vietnam from interfering in each other's affairs.

For Giap personally, the end of the Indo China war against the French must have been very welcome. A man of his upbringing would not have taken kindly to the privations of life

in the Viet Bac, and it is a fortunate general who can cease
fighting after the attainment of a great victory. Now the business was politics once more, and Giap could re-direct his
efforts to establishing the *Lao Dong* within North Vietnam,
with his influence enhanced by the after glow of a successful
campaign which never seems to harm a general with political
aspirations in any society. Nor did he have to turn to a completely new profession, for quite clearly the day of the soldier
in North Vietnam had entered on a period of siesta rather than
sunset, and at the early age of forty-two, Giap had a great deal
to look forward to. Perhaps, when he next took the field, he
would have an even greater role and a better basis for his
military strength than that which he was leaving behind.

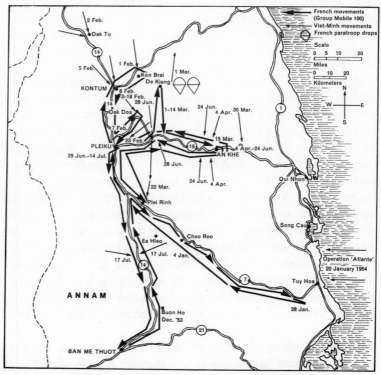

Military Operations, Central Highlands, 1954

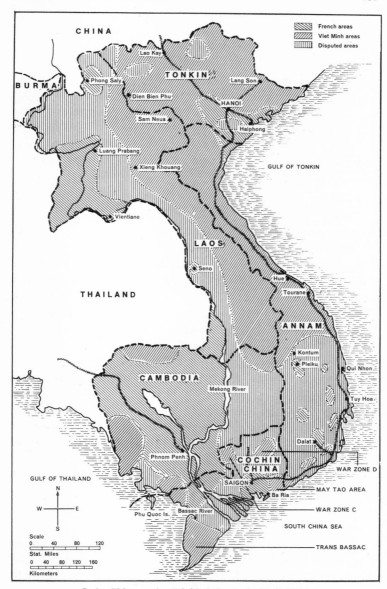

CHINA

Lao Kay

BURMA

Phong Saly

TONKIN

Dien Bien Phu

Lang Son

HANOI

Sam Neua

Haiphong

Luang Prabang

GULF OF TONKIN

Xieng Khouang

Vientiane

LAOS

THAILAND

Seno

Hue

Tourane

ANNAM

Kontum

Pleiku

Qui Nhon

CAMBODIA

Mekong River

Tuy Hoa

Dalat

Phnom Penh

COCHIN CHINA

WAR ZONE D

GULF OF THAILAND

SAIGON

MAY TAO AREA

Ba Ria

WAR ZONE C

Phu Quoc Is.

Bassac River

SOUTH CHINA SEA

TRANS BASSAC

French areas
Viet Minh areas
Disputed areas

N
W   E
S

Scale
0   40   80   120
Stat. Miles
0   40   80   120   160
Kilometers

Indo China under Divided Control, April 1954

9 Reformer and Author

During the months of the Geneva conference, the Viet Minh High Command took no risks of being captured by a desperate last French effort and they remained in the uncomfortable security of the Viet Bac until the agreed date of the French departure from Hanoi. The first groups of Viet Minh officials began to arrive in Hanoi on 3 October 1954 to commence their assumption of the administration of the city from the French. On 9 October the last French troops departed from Hanoi and the men of 308 Division entered with a ceremonial military parade on the following day. Despite the great exodus of businessmen, professors, members of the Vietnamese National Army and their dependants, there were still sufficient numbers of propertied Vietnamese in the crowds along the route of march to overlay the popular welcome with an air of apprehension. Some of these middle class representatives had an idea that the now unrestrainedly Communist Viet Minh regime would plunge North Vietnam into a sea of misery akin to that endured by the Soviet people between the two world wars.

The Viet Minh leaders did not arrive in Hanoi until several days later. Giap had been sent on ahead of Ho, and made his first appearance on 12 October, to inspect the Viet Minh guard at the Citadel which had replaced the French. This must have been a moment of which Giap had dreamed many times during the hardships, set backs and frustrations of life in the jungle during the previous eight years. However, the nature of his new duties soon showed itself as he hastened off to the power station to inspect arrangements which had been made with the French engineers who had agreed to stay on until the end of the year. Military matters were to occupy only a small part of Giap's time during the coming four years in which the foundation for a Communist society capable of enduring further stresses of war had to be laid.

Ho Chi Minh was first observed in Hanoi on 17 October at the arrival of North Vietman's first official visitor, Prime Minister Nehru of India, who was on his way to meet Chinese leaders in Peking. Official celebrations of victory were postponed until the commencement of the following year. In the presence of a crowd of 200,000 on 1 January 1955 Ho took the salute at an elaborate parade which went on for five and a half hours. The official party occupied a stand which was over sixty feet in height, adorned by an enormous portrait of Ho, before which countless Viet Minh units and sub-units, civilian and military, passed with waving flags, masses of flowers, pictures of Marx, Lenin, Stalin, Mao and other Communist leaders, and bearing slogans. Giap's maintenance of his status was illustrated by his inclusion with Ho and Pham Van Dong, then Foreign Minister, as the speechmakers of this supreme day in the history of the Democratic Republic of Vietnam.

In accordance with the Geneva agreement between the French and Viet Minh High Commands, the forces of each were to be regrouped to South and North Vietnam respectively within three hundred days. This did not require as great a movement of Viet Minh forces as of the French, because the greater part of the fighting had taken place in the North. Nonetheless, Giap had no intention of losing his hard won foothold in the South and instructions were given to local cadres to go underground for a period of a few years until their services were again required. Thus, despite the evacuation of most Viet Minh main force regiments and battalions from the South, the most important parts of their infra-structure were left intact.

The main force units, which normally lived apart from the people, in remote jungle bases from which they emerged at infrequent intervals to conduct raids and ambushes, were of little use in a direct political role such as that of the cadres. Probably Giap was happy to gather most of these units to North Vietnam for training in newer modes of warfare, more suited to the task of overthrowing an indigenous government.

The chaotic state of the South after the arrival of Ngo Dinh Diem to lead the government, and the opposition offered by the sects, notably the *Binh Xuyen*, made the tasks of the southern cadres relatively simple. The main Viet Minh base areas, War Zones C and D, north and north-east of Saigon respectively, Phuoc Tuy to the south-east, and the Trans-Bassac in the southernmost tip of Vietnam were not molested by the National troops and so it was an easy matter to conceal moderate supplies of arms, ammunition, sabotage materials and radio sets for future use. The fortifications were kept in some order, although not extended, and the curiosity of the Southern troops was discouraged by liberal distributions of boobytraps in the vacated bases. The main force units which re-grouped to North Vietnam contained mainly southerners, and thus Giap benefited by having several thousand troops with an intimate knowledge of many parts of South Vietnam who could set up a widespread intelligence network.

However, the emphasis of the Viet Minh in 1954-5 lay not in the direction of prosecuting a new war but in establishing their control over the gains of the war which had just ended. The major processes which they set in motion to achieve this control were: thought control, land rent reduction and land reform. Each of these campaigns overlapped during the period of greatest activity in the internal political field, 1953-6. Little is known of Giap's exact role in these programmes, which parts he directed, the differences he had with his colleagues, especially Truong Chinh, and which parts he had nothing to do with. We do know that he continued to be one of the most powerful of the Northern leaders and that therefore he bears great responsibility for the agonies which befell the North Vietnamese during these years. A brief examination of these years will serve to illustrate some of Giap's characteristics as a senior political leader.

The thought reform programme had begun in 1946, concentrating on the eradication of the elements of liberalism, such as individualism, romanticism, the notion of natural rights and tolerance of differences. French thought and culture was held to be particularly insidious and cancerous. The second phase of the thought reform campaign began in 1953, and was closely linked to the land rent reduction programme, attacking those traditions of thought which supported the notion of property, Confucianism, feudalism, and the age-old exploitation of tenants by landlords. During this phase, many non-Communists amongst those who had fought against the French were singled out for re-education, for punishment, and for unfavourable classification in the land reform programme.

The land rent reduction campaign took place during 1953 and 1954, serving as an introduction to the land reform programme. Both campaigns were aimed at the elimination of landowners as a class and the transfer of political power throughout the country to the lowest levels of the social structure, the landless peasant or the peasant who owned less than one acre and some hens. These peasants were the group least likely to place any obstacles in the path of the Party, while they were the only group whose assistance in eradicating the power of the middle classes could be relied on implicitly. The two campaigns worked on the divide and rule principle by first picking out the wealthier of the middle class elements for denunciation and trial while the remainder of the middle class tried to look as inconspicuous as possible for fear of identification with the wealthier group. Some went so far as to denounce their fellows in the hope of averting attention from themselves.

However, these measures did not satisfy the desires of the Party for complete mastery, and so the second phase was launched against the lower echelons of the middle class and the richer of the peasants. The land reform campaign began in 1954, paused during 1955 while emigration from North Vietnam was still permitted under the Geneva agreement, in order to avoid accelerating the outflow of population, and resumed in late 1955 and 1956. The most important organization during these years was the Party cadre which existed in every village and district. The cadres selected those who were to be stigmatized as landlords and arranged for other more fortunate peasants to be their denouncers. In extremes, close relatives were called upon where it was necessary to incriminate a man who had formerly had a very high standing in the local community. If a man had enjoyed a high moral reputation, then his daughter might have to denounce him for incest. A man who had been a patriotic supporter of the Viet Minh, whose sons had fought in the army, might be denounced by his wife for having signalled to a French aircraft.

Once a man or woman had been denounced, a debt which he owed to his village or his neighbours would be announced which had to be paid within a few days. This debt was calculated to amount to virtual confiscation of his goods and valuables. While this was going on, peasants had to attend classes where they were told of the crimes of the land-owning classes and each peasant had to denounce at least one crime committed by his own landlord. Any peasant who was hesitant to denounce his landlord was accused of sympathy for feudalism and was liable to denouncement himself for this offence. The denouncements took place in public, usually taking three days for each landlord or so-called landlord. Then followed the trials at which the landlords were not allowed to give evidence in their own defence because the only admissible evidence was the record of denunciation which the landlord had had to sign after the public humiliation. Sentences varied between imprisonment for five years and death, and most also involved total confiscation of the landlord's property. Members of a landlord's family usually suffered 'isolation' also, which meant that they were not allowed to work and that nobody else was allowed to supply them or communicate with them. A great many families simply died of starvation as a result.

The final costs and gains of the land reform programme are largely unknown. By 1956, so many of the peasants of North Vietnam had become frightened of the possibility of being branded as a landlord through having too much, that they contented themselves with working little above subsistence level. Overall agricultural production fell to disastrous levels. Somewhere in excess of 100,000 were killed during the implementation of the programme.[30] The gains to the landless seem to have been very meagre, largely because in the North, most of the land was owned in the form of small plots of from one to a few acres, while twenty per cent of the land was in the form of communal holdings. However, the campaigns achieved their intended purpose in terms of political effect, for by 1956 the grip of the *Lao Dong* encompassed every facet of village and town life and no Vietnamese felt safe to take any independent stand on matters which had been pronounced upon by the Party.

By mid 1956, signs of severe distress were beginning to appear throughout North Vietnam and it was clear that if the prevalent course were allowed to continue, the results would be irreparable damage to agriculture, to morale and to the standing of the *Lao Dong* generally throughout the country. The first indication that a reconsideration of the land reform policy was taking place at the highest level was given in an open letter of Ho Chi Minh to 'Compatriots in the Country' in which Ho admitted errors in the methods of the land reform and promised that rectifications would be made. On 24 August, the Party newspaper, *Nhan Dan*, stated that many former fighters for independence of the Vietnamese people had been wrongly

[30]The figure of 100,000 is given by Professor G. Tongas, who remained in Hanoi until 1959. A former Viet Minh sympathizer and now an anti-Communist, Tongas has recorded his observations of this period in: *J'ai vécu dans l'enfer communiste au Nord Viet-Nam et j'ai choisi la liberté* (Nouvelles Editions Debresse, Paris, 1960)

classified as enemies of the state and had been imprisoned or even executed.

The major announcements came in October 1956 when Ho dismissed the leader of the land reform programme, Truong Chinh, and the Minister for Agriculture, Ho Viet Thang. Ho assumed Truong Chinh's duties as Party Secretary until Le Duan took over in 1960. The official pronouncement of the Party on the subject was left to Giap to deliver. It is interesting that Ho did not do this himself—perhaps he felt that he had already given sufficient indication of his attitude in his open letter and that he would facilitate the rehabilitation of the former secretary by remaining somewhat aloof from the matter during the Party discussion. The task of proclaiming the evils of the land reform campaign in full was given to Giap, who made the following statement before the Tenth Congress of the Party Central Committee:

(a) While carrying out their anti-feudal task, our cadres have underestimated or, worse still, have denied all anti-imperialist achievements, and have separated the Land Reform and the Revolution. Worst of all, in some areas they have even made the two mutually exclusive.

(b) We have failed to realize the necessity of uniting with the middle-level peasants, and we should have concluded some form of alliance with the rich peasants, whom we treated in the same manner as landlords.

(c) We attacked the land owning families indiscriminately, according no consideration to those who have served the Revolution and to those families with sons in the army. We showed no indulgence towards landlords who participated in the Resistance, treating their children in the same way as we treated the children of other landlords.

(d) We made too many deviations and executed too many honest people. We attacked on too large a front and, seeing enemies everywhere, resorted to terror, which became far too widespread.

(e) Whilst carrying out our Land Reform programme we failed to respect the principles of freedom of faith and worship in many areas.

(f) In regions inhabited by minority tribes we have attacked tribal chiefs too strongly, thus injuring, instead of respecting, local customs and manners.

(g) When reorganizing the Party, we paid too much importance to the notion of social class instead of adhering firmly to the political qualifications alone. Instead of reorganizing education to be the first essential, we resorted exclusively to organizational measures such as disciplinary punishments, expulsion from the Party, executions, dissolution of Party branches and cells. Worse still, torture came to be regarded as a normal practice during Party reorganization.[31]

The misery which lay beneath the surface level on this iceberg can only be guessed at. For a government to confess to executing 'too many' honest people, to resorting to terror and using torture as a normal practice is astounding enough in itself, but this ought not to take the mind off the horrors committed. This had clearly been naked use of power to coerce the inhabitants of North Vietnam, and whatever the horrors of colonial administration had been in Tonkin and Annam, they fell far short of this admitted record. The mere fact that Giap remained a member of the inner cabinet which carried this policy into effect underlines the fundamental ruthlessness which he showed with regard to the lives of his troops between 1951 and 1954, and leads one to wonder whether, if Giap had had to operate within the restrictions which his opponents had to observe regarding human suffering, he would have been a successful general at all.

Shortly after the official announcement of the Campaign for the Rectification of Errors, whose very announcement may be taken as evidence that the situation had been brought under control, severe local disorders broke out in Nghe An province. The shock of these disturbances was magnified by two factors: Nghe An had been the birthplace of Communism in the North thirty years previously, and Ho Chi Minh himself had come from that province. Giap reacted quickly by sending in 325

[31]*Nhan Dan*, No. 970, 31 October 1956, quoted in Hoang Van Chi, *From Colonialism to Communism* (Frederick A. Praeger, New York, 1963), pp. 215-16 (popular edn.)

Division, the nearest of his main force formations, to suppress the revolts which were spreading spontaneously from district to district. The land reform measures were halted at once, but the fighting which took place was savage and bloody for nearly three weeks, from 2 November to 20 November, just at the time when the Soviets were putting down the Hungarian revolutionaries. Over one thousand peasants were killed or wounded, and over six thousand were deported before the authority of the *Lao Dong* had been restored. Several other disturbances occurred in late 1956, but details have not yet been allowed to filter through from Hanoi. Not until February 1957 was the North Vietnamese government confident enough to withdraw its regular troops from the troubled areas and restore local control to provincial and district forces.

Giap then set to with a complete reorganization of his command structure and of the training of the People's Army of North Vietnam (PAVN). The establishment of peaceful conditions enabled greater co-ordination of military training at the national, provincial, district and village levels, and conscription was maintained to allow the regular forces to be built up to twice the number of divisions which had fought the French. The foundations of the Naval and Air Forces of North Vietnam were also laid, with the assistance of the Soviet Union and China in providing equipment, instructors, technicians and in accepting large numbers of Vietnamese for training with their own armed forces.

It appears from this point of time that the North Vietnamese Government decided to engage in a further round of warfare in the late 1950s, with the aim of unifying Vietnam and thereby regaining the territory over which Ho had claimed to rule in August 1945. Too many factors are as yet unknown to permit a specific description of the outbreak of the second Indo China war, and therefore there is even less to be said about Giap's role in the conflict, short of the realm of speculation. However, the publication of some of his writings and speeches by the Hanoi regime in the 1960s has opened Giap to appreciation and criticism from some new points of view;

those of authorship and of creativity in terms of military theory.

The work for which he has become most widely known is *People's War People's Army*, published in Hanoi in 1961 in many languages, and aimed at those other revolutionaries who were, and still are, attempting to overthrow governments throughout Africa, Asia and Latin America. Because of the acclaim with which this publication has been received in many quarters—*Newsweek* described it as 'a classic manual on guerrilla warfare'—it calls for special comment.

People's War People's Army is a collection of speeches and articles written and delivered by Giap to mark special occasions in the life of the PAVN. They are, naturally, aimed at stimulating future actions on the part of Giap's troops rather than being a dispassionate exposition of a theory of warfare which the reader or listener may or may not accept, in whole or in part. The means used by Giap to arouse the devotion of his audience are chiefly adulation of the Party for its infallible leadership and glorification of the successes of the Viet Minh against the French. While neither of these means excludes the presentation of a new strategic or tactical doctrine as part of its content, it must be remembered that exhortatory speeches by successful generals have seldom made any significant contribution to the theory of warfare in the past.

Out of 217 pages, 27 are devoted to a brief résumé of events between 1930 and 1954. The next twenty-eight pages of text contain an article from which the book derives its title, written by Giap to mark the fifteenth anniversary of the PAVN. Then follow eighty-four pages of an article, *The Great Experiences Gained by Our Party In Leading The Armed Struggle And Building Revolutionary Armed Forces*, written to commemorate the thirtieth anniversary of the founding of the Indo China Communist Party. The final section contains sixty-five pages on Dien Bien Phu, being a re-print of a pamphlet published by Giap in 1959 to mark the fifth anniversary of his victory. The remaining thirteen pages are devoted to decorative effects by the publishers.

The first article describes the rise of the Communist movement within Vietnam, and the opening of hostilities with the French. Generally it is too brief to make many value judgements or to state any new piece of information regarding those events, but Giap was sufficiently unabashed to write of his period of office as Minister for the Interior in 1946:

> The liquidating of the reactionaries of the *Viet Nam Quoc Dan Dang* was crowned with success and we were able to liberate all the areas which had fallen into their hands.[32]

His references to the defeats of his divisions at the hands of de Lattre in 1951 are significant for their emptiness. He moves from 1950 to 1952 thus:

> In effect, 1950 marked the opening of a new phase in the evolution of our long Resistance. During the winter, in the frontier campaign, for the first time, we opened a relatively big counter-attack which resulted in the liberation of the provinces of Cao Bang, Lang Son and Lao Cai. Immediately after, we began a series of offensives on the delta front.
>
> The enemy, routed, sent General De Lattre de Tassigny to Indo China. The military aid granted by the United States following an agreement signed in 1950, was on the increase. The aggressive war waged by the French colonialists gradually became a war carried out with 'U.S. dollars' and 'French blood'. It was really a 'dirty war'.
>
> De Lattre's plan, approved by Washington, provided for a strong line of bunkers in the Red River delta to stop our progress, and for a regrouping of forces in order to launch violent mopping-up operations so as at all costs to 'pacify' the rear and create the right conditions for an offensive which would enable the French forces to recapture the initiative while attacking our free zone. In October 1951, the enemy occupied Hoa Binh. We replied by immediately launching the Hoa Binh campaign. On the one hand we contained and overwhelmed the adversary's forces on the 'opposite' front, on the other hand, we took advantage of their exposed disposition of troops to get our divisions to strike direct blows at their rear in the Red River delta. Our large guerrilla bases were extending further still, freeing nearly two

---

[32]Vo Nguyen Giap, *People's War People's Army, op. cit.*, p. 18

million inhabitants. Hoa Binh was released. De Lattre's plan was checked.

In 1952, we launched a campaign in the North-Western zone. . . .[33]

At no later stage does he return to make amplifying comment on the events of 1951. In describing the Navarre Plan, Giap attributes its authorship thus:

It was, in fact, the plan of the 'war-to-the-end' men, Laniel and Dulles.[34]

In view of what has become known about the origins of the Navarre Plan, this claim conflicts with the well established facts that not only was Laniel in favour of ending the war by negotiation in 1953, but he thought the Navarre Plan far too ambitious for Navarre's means—although he failed to make this clear to Navarre until after the catastrophe of 1954. Dulles was almost certainly aware of the major features of the Navarre Plan, but his subsequent vain efforts to obtain Congressional support for American intervention in Indo China at the height of the Dien Bien Phu battle incline one to believe that had he been one of the authors of the plan, then American support would have rested on a much firmer basis than it did in 1954.

After this chronological section, Giap concludes the article with some generalizations. The most severe problems which had to be overcome were the ensuring of a regular delivery of food for the fighting men and the conventional weaknesses of Giap's guerrillas and main force formations. He links the land reform campaign with the war against the French as being two parts of the one revolution.

The Vietnamese people's war of liberation brought out the importance of building resistance bases in the countryside and the close and indissoluble relationships between the anti-imperialist revolution and the anti-feudal revolution.[35]

[33]Giap, *op. cit.*, pp. 22-3
[34]Giap, *op. cit.*, p. 24
[35]Giap, *op. cit.*, p. 31. The italics are Giap's

In the face of the alleged importance of the co-ordination of land reform and the fighting against the French, Giap alludes to certain shortcomings of the former:

> Despite the errors which blemished its accomplishment, it was a correct line crowned with success. . . .[36]

and

> However, in the early years of the resistance a certain under-estimation of the importance of the peasant question hindered us from giving all the necessary attention to the worker-peasant alliance.[37]

The conventional weaknesses of the Viet Minh with respect to the French were overcome by the following formula:

> At an early stage, our Party was able to discern the character-istics of this war: a people's war and a long-lasting war, and it was by proceeding from these premises that, during the whole of hostilities and in particularly difficult conditions, the Party solved all the problems of the Resistance.[38]

This conclusion follows two pages of preamble which bear out the logical correctness of the conclusion, but it is pertinent to ask exactly what Giap meant by 'at an early stage': did he wish to imply that the Party had discerned that the war would have to be a protracted struggle in 1951? If it had, why were the offensives launched against the Red River delta, and why where Viet Minh propagandists proclaiming 'Ho Chi Minh in Hanoi for *Tet*'? Giap offers no defence to the charge that he hoped for a quick victory over the French and that he had to fall back on protracted warfare because the only other course open to him was surrender.

The article finishes with a eulogy of the Party and of its leadership—possibly this is the only way in which Giap could emulate some of the greater self-justifications written by Lord

[36]*Ibid*
[37]Giap, *op. cit.*, p. 33
[38]Giap, *op. cit.*, p. 28

Montgomery—but nonetheless it makes a distasteful impression to read sentences such as:

> The Vietnamese people's war of liberation attained this great victory for the reasons we have just enumerated, but above all because it was *organized and led by the Party of the working class: the Indochinese Communist Party, now the Viet Nam Workers' Party.*[39]

The contribution of international Communism to the victories of the Viet Minh is also acknowledged:

> If the Vietnamese people's war of liberation ended in a glorious victory, it is because we did not fight alone, but with the *support of progressive peoples the world over, and more especially the peoples of the brother countries with the Soviet Union at the head.* The victory of the Vietnamese people cannot be divided from this support; it cannot be disassociated from the brilliant successes of the socialist countries and the movement of national liberation, neither can it be detached from the victories of the Soviet Red Army during the Second World War, nor from those of the Chinese people during the last few years. It cannot be isolated from the sympathy and support of progressive peoples throughout the world, among whom are the French people under the leadership of their Communist Party, and the peoples of Asia and Africa.[40]

Despite the obvious diplomacy of these comments, and the precedence given to the Soviet Union rather than China, there is more behind these words than mere international politeness. Unless the Chinese really fall out with the Vietnamese regime in Hanoi, we shall never know the full measure of Chinese advice and assistance to the Viet Minh—nor shall we know how many 'ugly Chinamen' blundered paternalistically amongst people of whom they knew little.

The article *People's War People's Army* is a variation on the first article, containing a résumé of the Indo China war, an outline history of the PAVN emphasising the leadership of

[39]Giap, *op. cit.*, p. 35. The italics are Giap's
[40]Giap, *op. cit.*, p. 36. The italics are Giap's

the Party and another eulogy of the Party. The title is apt, because the first section described the outlines of a people's war and the second describes the growth of a people's army. Neither section makes any further contribution to military theory than the first article. In the section on the PAVN, Giap poses a paradox:

> Since the return of peace, it has been necessary to replace voluntary service by *compulsory military service*. This substitution has met with a warm response from the population.[41]

The third article is a three part eulogy of the Party, ostensibly written to celebrate the thirtieth anniversary of the foundation of the Indo Chinese Communist Party, but its blatancy suggests that Giap may have had another motive, possibly connected with his internal standing in the Hanoi hierarchy.

The first section of the article is entitled *Our Party Successfully Led the Preparation For The Armed Uprising And The August 1945 General Insurrection*. It covers the major activities of the Party between 1939 and 1945, but in too general a way to be of more than incidental value to a student of these events. The second section is headed *Our Party Victoriously Led The Long-Term Resistance War Against The French Imperialists And U.S. Interventionists*, and offers yet another summary of events between 1945 and 1954. Points which are mentioned specially are: the policy of forming a united nationalist front by alliances with other parties in the early years of the war, the continuing emphasis on land reform throughout these years as a part of the Party's platform, and a Maoist analysis of the strategic problems which led to the adoption of the notions of protracted war, people's war and the various stages through which such a war has to advance before the final offensive can be launched.

The third section, *Our Party Has Successfully Led The Building Of The People's Revolutionary Armed Forces*, de-

---

[41]Giap, *op. cit.*, p. 62. The italics are Giap's

scribes the brilliance of Party leadership in the post 1954 period which saw the transformation of the war-torn divisions of the previous years into the well equipped and well regulated PAVN. The three sub-sections stress that the Army was successful because of its ideology and complete subordination to Party leadership, that the Party laid the proper political foundations and guide lines for the political growth of the Army, and that the Party has solved all questions of administration necessary to convert a guerrilla army into a modern regular army. Presumably Giap has become aware that guerrilla warfare is not sufficient in itself to achieve a military result when faced by an opponent who can maintain an appreciable conventional military strength.

Both the second and the third sections of this article contain discussions of strategy and tactics and are valuable in that they show conclusively that the Viet Minh adopted most of the doctrines of the Chinese Communists, and that their army was organized along normal lines for a Communist force. As a re-emphasis of Maoist ideas and as a reminder of the ways in which Communist insurgents fight, they are well worth reading, just as American versions of the notions of Sir Robert Thompson can be. However, to claim that they contain new, even revolutionary, ideas is to make a serious exaggeration. This is not to say that Giap himself has never thought out any striking and original ideas on the subject of warfare. All that can be said is that if he has, he has never published them abroad, which is, after all, only a wise policy for a man who is still fighting a long and difficult war.

The fourth part of *People's War People's Army*, Giap's account of the battle of Dien Bien Phu, is an important piece of historical writing in which Giap lays bare the central problems, both strategic and tactical, which confronted him and describes the answers he gave to them. He includes enough of his reasoning to give the reader a very clear idea of what was in his mind during the various stages of the struggle, and from this reasoning, his stature as a highly developed practitioner of the military arts emerges.

The section opens with short discussions of the strategic and tactical considerations which led him to respond in full array to the French challenge. The problems of overcoming the French defence are outlined and then, as befits a commemorative article, a long concluding chapter follows, praising the determination of the Army, the devotion of the people in serving the front line troops, and moralizing that the entire war for the liberation of the Vietnamese people was 'one long and great Dien Bien Phu battle'. In this claim, Giap shows himself in no worse a light than many other leaders who continue to eulogize the spirit of Dunkirk and Valley Forge.

The appendix which Giap has attached to the fourth section provides further important details chiefly concerned with the tactical problems of storming the French defences at Dien Bien Phu. His counters to the Navarre Plan are also described but the repetitive nature of this appendix suggests that it was written as a separate piece from the main part of the section, possibly for a different purpose, and then tacked on to make weight for the book. Had this section been edited, a great deal of disconnected repetition could have been placed in chronological sequence to give a most interesting and moderately detailed account of the development of the final nine months of the war.

From this examination of the content of *People's War People's Army*, it may be seen that Giap did not take the opportunity afforded by its publication to make a reputation for himself as an original strategic or tactical thinker. However, he (or his research staff) has proved to be a coherent narrator of complicated events and processes with an eye to the historical importance of the events in which he has been involved. If political circumstances ever permitted, there is little doubt that Giap could produce a work of much higher quality.

People's War People's Army is far from being Giap's only claim to authorship but is the nearest approach he has made to portraying the details of the event in which he is involved in an objective manner. Other works such as *Once Again We*

Will Win, published in 1966, and *Big Victory, Great Task*, which followed in 1967, are little more than the propaganda which their titles suggest. These volumes are collections of articles written by Giap for *Nhan Dan* and *Quan Doi Nhan Dan*, and their purpose appears to be to boost North Vietnamese morale at a time of severe stress due to the American bombing. To a specialist in propaganda studies, these articles are of considerable importance, for they show the methods of current operational Asian Communism, but they have little to add to an understanding of Giap's life in themselves, except to show that the propagandist of the late 1930s has not lost the skills which brought him to power.

10 The Second Indo-China War

Since 1957 Giap has been engaged in events which by themselves are of sufficient significance to ensure him a place in
world history as a military and political leader of great importance. His role in the direction of the war which is still
raging in Vietnam and which is having the deepest political
repercussions in the U.S.A. has appeared to have been so
skilfully executed that he has emerged as the leading military
figure of the war—a commander who has kept his post
throughout the conflict while the leaders of his enemies have
risen and fallen several times over.

Because the war drags on however the Hanoi government
has maintained a strict barrier of security against outside attempts to probe the details of Giap's role in the formation of
strategy and in the conduct of operations. There have been
many rumours concerning Giap's activities, such as one current in late 1967 that he was present when the North Vietnamese divisions were besieging Khe Sanh and was exercising
personal command of the battle in the hope of achieving
another Dien Bien Phu. But in the absence of confirmatory
statements from Hanoi, there is little that can be said in detail
about his part in the war. Until we know whether or not he did
control forward Viet Cong and North Vietnamese operations
in a tactical sense, and until the extent of his influence in the
higher policy-forming bodies in Hanoi is known, we cannot

178

analyse his role in any depth. All that can be done with confidence at this point of time, i.e. March 1969, is to outline Giap's place in the structure of North Vietnamese politics, to describe a few incidents involving him which were not completely hidden from the outside world, and with whatever perspective may be available at this close point of c^hservation, to examine the strategy of the Viet Cong and North Vietnamese since 1957 on the assumption that Giap has continued to carry overall military responsibility for actions initiated in Hanoi or at Hanoi's behest.

North Vietnam is organized politically as a presidentially-directed state in which, as in the Fifth French Republic, the President has far-reaching powers and the Prime Minister is merely the first of the president's ministers. The first constitution of 1946 was in form a more liberal document than its successor, the 1960 constitution. The latter reflects possibly the feeling of confidence of an established government in its ability to maintain an absolute degree of control over the political behaviour of its subject citizens. However, the constitution represents the shadow rather than the substance of the North Vietnamese political system, for as in all Communist states, effective power is a monopoly of the Communist Party, in this case since 1951 called the *Lao Dong*.

Ho Chi Minh's grasp on political power is indicated by his possession of the offices of both Chairman of the *Lao Dong* and President of the Democratic Republic of Vietnam. Beneath him in the two hierarchies are the Politburo of the Party and the Cabinet of Ministers. The prime roles in these two bodies are assigned to Le Duan as Party Secretary and to Pham Van Dong as Prime Minister. Although Giap has failed to gain either of these posts, he has collected an impressive total of offices—member of the Politburo, Deputy Premier, Minister of Defence and Commander in Chief of the People's Army of Vietnam. Although his political fortunes may have risen and fallen since 1957, Giap has continued to enjoy wide powers and has held membership of the highest councils of North Vietnam. Given this opportunity to express his views, it would seem most improbable that the man who ousted the French is treated with anything other than deference and respect within the Politburo and the Cabinet and therefore it seems that North Vietnamese strategy, at least, has been largely in his hands.

During 1957 Giap disappeared from public view for some months and fears were held by his friends in the outside world that he had been removed from office. Whatever the explanation of this absence from public view, he came back to prominence in 1958 at a time when North Vietnam was beginning to recover from the disasters of land reform and to grapple with the problem of the overthrow of Diem and re-unification with the South.

The origins of wars pose some of the most complicated of all historical questions. Despite the availability of huge quantities of official documents, private memoirs and secret papers relating to the causes of both world wars, the debates on these subjects have continued to rage with a ferocity quite unabated during the passage of many years. From the nature of war, where at least the loser suffers very badly, the historian looks for both a 'war party' and an 'anti-war party' on the defeated side because presumably at least some small group of people on that side had the prudence to foresee the possibility of their defeat. The peculiarly devastating nature of modern war has made abundantly clear, since 1915 at least, that victory is unlikely to be won cheaply and that a victor must assume, for the sake of his long term security, post-war economic obligations towards the defeated. Consequently it seems reasonable for the historian to look for 'war parties' and 'anti-war parties' amongst all contenders. However the importance of public opinion in war and the development of mass communications media which can mobilize this opinion have placed enormous obstacles in the historian's path towards truth. The effect of wartime propaganda is heightened by the relative monopoly of post war propaganda exercised by victor nations and it is frequently very difficult for any historian to know whether in the course of his investigations he is being swept to one side or the other by the conditioning he has suffered from war propaganda.

In the light of the evidence currently available relating to the outbreak of the second Indo China war and in view of the impassioned clash of rival propaganda, it would be very rash to attempt an analysis of the causes of this war, of the aims of the opponents in using military force, and of the degree to which the leaders of the warring nations are to be morally condemned or commended. However there are some interim observations which can be made from this short perspective of ten years.

After the Geneva conference of 1954, the Viet Minh regime and its supporters felt that they had been cruelly cheated of the rightful fruits of their hard-won victory through being confined to Tonkin and Northern Annam when they claimed, with some justification, to represent nationalists throughout Vietnam and when in fact for a brief period after the Japanese collapse in 1945, they had ruled over the entire Vietnamese nation. Whether they really believed that the free elections supposed to be carried out in 1956 could ever take place is not known. The North Vietnamese made much of Diem's unwillingness to hold these elections but it seems unlikely that men with the political acumen of Ho Chi Minh and Pham Van Dong would imagine Diem to have so naive as to commit political suicide. Nonetheless, the North Vietnamese exploited this incident to the full, both in internal politics and in the international sphere. It was made plain to the world that North Vietnam did not accept the Seventeenth Parallel as a permanent boundary and that it desired to eliminate the Saigon regime. What was not obvious was whether the North Vietnamese were prepared to go to war over the issue or rely on internal forces working within South Vietnam to topple Diem in favour of a Communist takeover.

Diem, a leader with autocratic tendencies and an acute awareness of the insecurity of his regime, reacted strongly to any suspected Communist threats by suppressing them with considerable force. Often this force was wrongly applied and Diem made enemies of many who were far from Communist in their beliefs. Diem's forces were too efficient to be ignored, yet lacked the power to control the whole countryside. Consequently, opposing groups were forced to flee to remote parts of South Vietnam, where they were able to organize themselves into armed units with the assistance of some North Vietnamese cadres and military equipment captured from Diem's forces. Minor clashes occurred in 1958 and by 1959, Diem had a severe internal security problem on his hands caused by local insurrection. The notion of compromise being totally abhorrent to him, he stepped up his efforts to crush the insurgents, and in the process alienated many more South Vietnamese who felt that they were being terrorized by a dictatorship.

Before responsibility for escalating the war to a major conflict can be placed on Diem's shoulders however, it is only fair to ask whether the growth of insurgency in South Vietnam was a response to his methods of rule or the result of North Vietnamese instigation. We know that some Viet Minh cadres were left behind in the South when Communist forces were regrouped to the North, so there is some evidence of North Vietnamese interference in the affairs of the South. However we also know that a sizable proportion of Diem's opponents were not Communists and that they had no ties with the North. Hence we have a situation in which many forces were working, and there is no simple answer as to who caused the escalation into war in Vietnam in 1959 and 1960. The difficulties of this problem have not daunted the theorists of either side and reams of evidence have been produced to lay the blame on either Diem or Ho. The point which seems to have been overlooked in the debate is that possibly each side felt its legitimate interests and security to be threatened by the activities of the other, and felt forced to match an eye for an eye, adding a certain margin for safety, thereby breeding an inherently unstable situation which had to escalate until the limits of the resources of both North and South were reached.

Once that point appeared to be approached for either side, then it was up to that government's allies to decide whether to add their support or not and to what extent.

Whatever the causes of the war, the North Vietnamese leaders found themselves in a dilemma regarding their policy towards events in the South. The Soviet policy stressed peaceful co-existence to the other Communist states as a principle of foreign relations, while Chinese policy pressed for strong action against Imperialists and Paper Tigers. North Vietnam had close links with both great powers and could afford to offend neither through her action or lack of it against the South. The deepening of rivalry between the Soviet Union and China greatly complicated this task although it also meant that neither of the two leading Communist powers could afford, for the sake of its prestige within the Communist bloc, to appear to desert North Vietnam if it got into difficulties.

Ho evidently regarded the best policy to follow as one of delicate compromise between his two major allies, as has been seen from his actions since 1960; but this concept did not appear to be the wisest as far as two of his senior lieutenants were concerned, and a long standing rivalry was fanned from smouldering embers to dangerous flames.

Truong Chinh, number three man in the Politburo next to Ho and Party Secretary Le Duan, military theorist and former Party Secretary until 1956, received his early training in China and has tended both to share the views of Mao and to place prime importance in foreign policy on the link with Peking. In view of the assistance provided by the Chinese from 1950 to 1954, there seems to be much to be said for Truong Chinh's view. To Giap, however the relationship with China seemed fraught with perils which needed to be offset by assiduous courting of the Soviet Union. From his student days, Giap was well acquainted with the earlier history of Vietnam as a client state, tributary and even province of China, and he saw that Vietnamese independence of China was more exceptional than normal and that this dependence usually worked very much to the disadvantage of the Vietnamese. While there was some rivalry between China and the Soviet Union there appeared to him to be much sense in promoting ties with the Soviet Union and thereby preserving independence of either great power.

A natural rivalry had existed between Giap and Truong Chinh for many years. Giap's intellectual background and tastes exposed him to charges of bourgeois inclinations, while Truong Chinh's stance could be classified as on the left wing of the Party. Both men had appreciable military talents—Chinh had written a better book than Giap on revolutionary warfare, and Giap had won renown as a field commander. They were natural competition for one another. Each had a large personal following of important persons—Chinh had the Party while Giap had the Army. In 1950, Chinh had accused Giap of choosing subordinates who were unreliable and had been able to have one of them, Tran Chi Chau, head of the military supply service, executed.

After the Geneva settlement in 1954, Giap's prestige began to wane a little as North Vietnam settled into an era of internal reform. The influence of the Chinese grew as the nature of their assistance changed from military to economic, with deliveries of large quantities of machinery, raw materials and consumer goods, the service of advisors and the availability of large grants and loans for development. Truong Chinh's status was high as a result and Giap seemed to be a spent force. However, the disasters of the land reform which had been associated with Truong Chinh served to reverse this trend in 1956. As part of the Rectification of Errors campaign, Chinh had to resign from the secretaryship of the Party and publicly confess his mistakes while Giap gained much approval for his part in the denunciation of the excesses of the land reforms. However it is interesting that Chinh was not made a complete scapegoat and expelled from the senior ranks of the Party but was allowed to continue his membership of the Politburo. The force of Giap's rivalry was not sufficient to banish Chinh from the political scene.

During Ho's absence abroad in late 1957, Truong Chinh came back to prominence while Giap disappeared for a few months. Pro-China policies were stressed to the people until Ho returned home, possibly after Chinh had promised to support Ho's general policy of impartiality.

After the return of Ho, Giap returned gradually to prominence and took the lead at the end of the year in a curious incident known as the Phu Loi affair. Phu Loi internment camp had been established by Diem's government to hold Viet Cong prisoners. It lay some two miles from Thu Dau Mot city and twenty miles north of Saigon, so the conduct of affairs at the camp could be investigated by foreign journalists rather easily. North Vietnamese interest in the camp was finally revealed on 18 January 1959 when Giap sent the following 'most urgent' letter to the Chairman of the International Control Commission, Mr S. S. Ansari of India, at his office in Saigon. The letter contained the following:[42]

Disguised under the name of 'Central Political Re-education Centre', the Phu Loi internment camp in Phu Hoa village, Chau Thanh district, Thu Dau Mot province is the biggest concentration camp in the system of prisons and places of detention in south Viet Nam, which has been the subject of many letters from the Viet Nam People's Army side to the International Commission.

In June 1958, about 6,000 prisoners of both sexes were concentrated there; brought in from prisons and places of detention at Con Lon (Poulo Condor), Chi Hoa, Phu Quoc and elsewhere, they are for the most part former resistance members and patriots from all walks of life and of different political beliefs who desire peace, national reunification and the execution of the Geneva Agreements.

The south Viet Nam authorities have enforced in this camp an extremely harsh prison system, resulting in a sick rate running regularly into the thousands and a monthly death rate of hundreds.

[42]The full text of Giap's letter has been published in Malcolm Salmon, *Focus on Indo-China*, Foreign Languages Publishing House, Hanoi, 1961, pp. 184-6

Not content with such methods of murder, in the early days of December 1958, they ordered the mass poisoning of prisoners. After the poisoned meal, over 1,000 people died and thousands of others were seriously ill. A number of them who attempted to climb on to roofs to shout for help were shot down by prison guards. Over the following days the authorities sent a regiment to encircle the camp and a civil guard force to bar access to it; they then had petrol brought and set fire to the prison buildings, causing more deaths and incinerating many corpses of poison victims. Thousands of people from nearby villages, including parents and relatives of victims, rushed repeatedly to their rescue, but they were held back by the armed agents of the south Viet Nam authorities.

Following the mass murders of former resistance members at Duy Xuyen and Huong Dien in 1955, already known to the International Commission, this is the most cruel massacre recorded so far in the 'denounce and wipe out communists' policy of the south Viet Nam administration, a policy which amounts in essence to taking reprisals against former members of the resistance, and repressing patriots in south Viet Nam, in execution of the scheme to perpetuate Viet Nam's partition and to turn south Viet Nam into an American colony and base for war preparation in South-east Asia. . . .

The validity of Giap's charges is perhaps best indicated by a few words from Philippe Devillers, a French scholar and writer who is not noted for any friendship towards the Diem regime. Devillers writes:[43]

In December 1958, the death of some 20 Viet Cong detainees in the Phu Loi concentration camp served to flame the anger of the guerillas—and gave Hanoi an opportunity for propaganda— and to bring them to the point where they decided to answer force by force.

Obviously Giap was lending his name in this letter to nothing more than crude propaganda, but this aspect is the least important of the whole incident. As Devillers has stated, the Phu Loi affair gave Hanoi an opportunity to stir up feelings

[43]Philippe Devillers, 'The Struggle for Unification', in P. J. Honey, ed., *North Vietnam Today, Profile of a Communist Satellite*, Frederick A. Praeger, New York, 1962, p. 37

against the Diem government both north and south of the Seventeenth Parallel and this opportunity was exploited to the full. In the words of the North Vietnamese Government:[44]

> In January 1959, millions of people everywhere held meetings and demonstrations in protest against the massacre at the Phu Loi concentration camp. In Hanoi alone, on January 25, 1959, 300,000 people turned out in the streets and took part in a protest march, demanding that the Southern authorities disband their concentration camps. Many people went into mourning for the Southern victims. Within a week, 500 delegations of people's representatives came to the headquarters of the International Commission and handed in protests against the massacres of Southern patriots by U.S. imperialism and Diem. Recently the Northern people have started the 'sworn brotherhood' movement with the populations of the Southern provinces. This movement is of deep significance in uniting the people of the two zones in the struggle for national unity.

If one can speak of a *casus belli* in the tangle of events which led to the outbreak of hostilities organized on a large scale in South Vietnam, then the Phu Loi affair is as close as one may get. During January 1959 and in the months following, guerrilla attacks on the Government's forces, officials and installations began throughout South Vietnam. The major Viet Cong base areas of the Central Highlands, War Zones C and D and Cape Ca Mau were expanded and protected through seizure of many of the villages in and around them. The initiative and strength of these early operations was in the hands of Southern dissidents rather than with Ho Chi Minh in Hanoi, but the opportunity offered by the growth of violence in the South to achieve re-unification under Communist rule was too tempting for the Northern regime to remain a mere onlooker.

Deciding how far to support revolution in the South was not an easy matter for the Politburo. Soviet leadership of the Communist bloc was still effective and the policy laid down from the Kremlin demanded the avoidance of military conflicts

[44]As published in the official handbook *The Democratic Republic of Viet Nam*, Foreign Languages Publishing House, Hanoi, 1960, p. 133.

which were liable to lead eventually to a confrontation between the Soviet Union and the United States. In the light of this policy it is possible to discern both a war party and an anti-war party in Hanoi. As may be expected from the nature of the divisions already existing within the leadership of the *Lao Dong*, Truong Chinh was actively espousing a Maoist line of full support for the revolutionaries while Giap counselled adherence to a more moderate line which would not involve the North directly in war.

In view of Giap's initiative in creating the stir about the Phu Loi incident and in deliberately inflaming opinion in the North against Diem, his pursuit of a moderate policy may seem strange. However, it must be remembered that the Geneva agreements between the French and the Viet Minh were made between the military commanders of the two governments and that hence, in the case of complaints to the International Control Commission, Giap formed the appropriate diplomatic link. He may well have had some reservations about the message which he had been required to pass to the Commission but had been overruled. Even had Giap been an instigator of the Communist propaganda, he could have been sufficiently out of touch with the feeling of the Southern opponents of Diem to imagine that the incident would have political rather than military repercussions.

During 1959, Giap gathered together several of his best pieces of strategic writing and published them with a little expansion in the following year. In the light of the strategic debate going on in Hanoi at that time it seems impossible that Giap's now famous book *People's War People's Army* was published without some intention to influence overall Communist policy in Vietnam and to consolidate support behind the commander in chief. The book itself has already been discussed, but its reiteration of the three classical phases of revolutionary war and of the doctrine of protracted war deserves special emphasis. Giap believed that Diem could not be overthrown in a short space of time and that victory could be achieved only by proceeding carefully through each of the three phases and by allowing sufficient time to plan the development of each phase before action was begun.

While Giap was pleading the case for a protracted war strategy, Truong Chinh was building up support for a more attractive policy—that of a general uprising or classic urban revolution based on the French and Russian models. His notion was that the people of South Vietnam would, with appropriate encouragement and assistance, rise up in a body and eject the Diem regime through a total refusal to co-operate with it. This doctrine was based on an over-optimistic appraisal of public feeling in the South through ignoring what Truong Chinh found difficult to perceive—that many Southerners, even amongst Diem's opponents, knew enough about the nature of the Northern government to be most reluctant to risk creating a situation in which Hanoi could take over the South.

The theory of the general uprising became the mainstay of Northern strategy until 1963, when even the fall of Diem did not lead to a Communist seizure of power and the hollowness of the theory was proved. Although the *Lao Dong* put faith in the general uprising and continued to provide cadres and training facilities for the Southern rebels, they were careful not to offend the Russians through any more direct commitment to the struggle. Chinese pressure to increase support for the war built up in 1960, particularly at the time of the Third Conference of the *Lao Dong* in September, but the Politburo did not go far beyond the political field—believing of course for the most part that political support was all that was necessary to enable the Southern Communists to replace Diem.

In December 1960, the National Liberation Front was set up in the South to direct the insurgency against the government. The Front was mainly South Vietnamese in composition but despite the great variety of political opinion amongst those who opposed Diem, was effectively dominated by Communists. The leaders were from the South, but they were assisted by others who had been living in the North since 1954. The degree to which Hanoi was responsible for founding the Front is un-

certain at the present time but there has been a constant flow
of men, money and supplies from the North to sustain the
Front's activities. As the war dragged on and more of the
Southern insurgents were eliminated by the South Vietnamese
and American action, the flow of aid from the North increased
and the strategic initiative on the Communist side passed
directly to Hanoi.

The apparent failure of the general uprising approach did
much to transfer power to the hands of Giap in 1964 although
it did not prevent the activists from attempting to accelerate
Giap's programme for passing through the three phases of the
protracted guerrilla war. During 1964, the scale of warfare in
the South advanced to that of full regimental attacks by over
2,000 soldiers, on Government posts and communications
routes. The amount of supplies and equipment needed to sustain this level of warfare was not to be had merely from capturing South Vietnamese stocks, and large quantities of ammunition, medical supplies and weapons were supplied by the
North. The Viet Cong, still at this stage mainly Southerners,
numbered several divisions, most of which had three regiments
of infantry. These regulars were backed up by other regular
units in the provinces—the provincial mobile battalions—
and by the district guerrilla companies, the village guerrilla
platoons and the hamlet guerrilla squads.

The chaotic political conditions in Saigon following the
coup against Diem did much to weaken the Southern efforts
and the South Vietnamese Army, never well trained and
organized, began to crumble. Clearly victory was now a feasible prospect for the insurgents, provided that it could be
achieved without provoking massive American military
involvement. Giap stepped up the pace of operations in a bid
to cut the South into two pieces for easy digestion. The Viet
Cong forces in the Central Highlands began to make a thrust
from the Central Mountain Chain towards the coast in the
vicinity of Pleiku and An Khe, the scene of another bid to
divide the South by the Communists ten years earlier. Had the
Viet Cong been able to achieve more rapid successes, there is

a strong chance that the commitment of large numbers of American troops to the war would have come too late. However, this was not to be. Viet Cong successes continued to mount, but the rate of disintegration of the South Vietnamese Army was not sufficient to allow the Viet Cong to achieve their goal before the close of 1964. In the meantime, the danger signals had begun to ring in several quarters in Washington and President Johnson authorized the dispatch of large ground forces to retrieve the situation and to give the South Vietnamese a little time to catch their breath. The Gulf of Tonkin incident had also occurred and North Vietnam became a target for the U.S. Air Force to bomb and strafe. At this point the wisdom of Giap's policy of protracted war became apparent. Having missed their best opportunity, the Viet Cong had little to look forward to but a long struggle with the forces of the United States.

Giap no doubt realized that the North Vietnamese were not entirely at a disadvantage by comparison with the United States in such a conflict. The North Vietnamese were certainly far weaker than the United States in materials of war, weapons and supply systems but in a political sense they had a great advantage—control over public opinion. Giap had seen how the French had grown tired of their war with the Viet Minh as it dragged on year after year and he was fully aware of the latent forces in American society which would combine to resist a long term American commitment to an inconclusive war. Giap has expressed his belief in the forces of public opinion thus:[45]

It is obvious that our Vietnamese people have sufficient determination and capabilities and will certainly and completely defeat the U.S. invaders' war of aggression. In the fierce fight against the U.S. aggressors, the most cruel and barbarous imperialist ringleaders of the present war, our Vietnamese people will certainly achieve complete victory, because our great national

[45]Vo Nguyen Giap, *Big Victory, Great Task*, Frederick A. Praeger, New York, 1968, p. 119. This volume reproduces a series of articles by Giap published in *Nhan Dan* and *Quan Doi Nhan Dan*, Hanoi, 14-16 September 1967

salvation resistance has been glowing with just cause, has enjoyed
correct political and military doctrine and the united strength of
our people who rose up to struggle, has possessed a firm determination and skilled fighting methods, and has enjoyed great
assistance from the brotherly socialist countries and strong
sympathy and encouragement from progressive people of the
world, including the American people.

Apart from the political benefits of fighting a protracted war
against a country which permits open dissent from government
policy, it is very likely that Giap saw from his experience
against the French an economic factor which would place
severe limitations on the effectiveness of American support for
the Southern government. As far as the average American
citizen was concerned, who ruled South Vietnam was of no
direct importance, save in somewhat clouded moral terms.
Adjusting the finer weights on the balance of power might meet
with general American approval, but only to the extent that
the American public were not required to meet any financial
burdens apart from a moderate increase in taxation. Thus, provided that Giap could prevent the occurrence of any severe
provocation of American public opinion such as the entry of
Chinese troops into the war, he could reckon on fighting an
America which was not mobilized.

It is unlikely that he ever hoped that the Americans would
shun, as did the French, the use of conscripts in Vietnam, but
even with conscription it was most improbable that they could
field an army of greater than 600,000 against him. With nearly
500,000 South Vietnamese troops to add to these, the military
balance was still tolerable for Giap. There were nearly
200,000 Viet Cong under arms in the South and of his own
army of some 500,000, he could field at least 100,000 troops
in the operational areas. Thus he had to cope with a numerical
superiority of only three to one—a ratio which his experience
had shown him was more than adequate for sustaining a protracted guerrilla war. Even if all the troops and commanders
opposing him were first class it would essentially be a matter
of outlasting the Americans and in view of the great strength

of the North Vietnamese control over the Communist movement in Vietnam, this prospect must have offered fair chances
for success.

Although the main emphasis in Northern strategy was on a
war of long duration, this was not to say that Giap should not
prepare to make the most of whatever opportunities arose to
exploit the weaknesses and shortcomings of his enemies. The
failure of the attempt to split South Vietnam into two, and
the influx of American troops which began in 1965, dictated a
selection of an entirely different sort of goal. Leaving the
central regions of South Vietnam, he turned his attention to
the area around the Demilitarized Zone and immediately south
of it and to Saigon, the trouble-rent capital which was sustaining the war in the South. The most northern sector of
South Vietnam is generally known as I Corps area, and was
selected by Giap because of the ease of direct communication
with the North. In I Corps area, he could maintain several
divisions of troops engaged in major battles. Although the
Americans enjoyed advantages of air power and mobility, they
could not achieve any great numerical preponderance over the
North Vietnamese in this area without gravely weakening their
hold on other parts of South Vietnam.

Plans for an assault on Saigon had been considered for some
time, and three Viet Cong divisions had been formed within
fifty miles of the capital, based in War Zones C and D, and in
Phuoc Tuy province. Given a period of two years, it was
hoped by the Viet Cong High Command and by Giap that
these divisions would gradually isolate Saigon from the surrounding countryside. They would then mount a three-pronged
assault on the city to physically eject the South Vietnamese
government and install the National Liberation Front in office.

Both of these plans had the strategic advantage to Giap of
dispersing the American effort and of getting them heavily
involved in jungle warfare where they would face the Viet
Cong forces on ground of the latter's own choosing. Thereby
the American loss rate would be maximized and so lead most
quickly to the growth of American public pressures for an

end to the war. While the Americans were involved in mobile warfare in the more remote parts of South Vietnam, the way was left open for the Viet Cong to deploy their strongest weapon—the cadres who infiltrated the villages and towns to work on popular discontent and to win mass support for the aims of the National Liberation Front. Provided these cadres could continue to work, chances that Viet Cong strength would grow were high. As soon as they were eliminated, the Viet Cong regiments and battalions would find themselves short of re-inforcements, supplies and information, while government authority in the villages and towns would meet much less of a challenge. However, with the main Allied effort being put into operations aimed at eliminating the Viet Cong main force units, the cadres were able to function and negate much of the Allied gains through sweep operations.

The theory of the three stage guerrilla war dominated Viet Cong activities from 1965 to 1967. Giap cautiously adjusted the level of the war in each of the Corps areas to suit local conditions. In I Corps area his forces fought at the third level of large scale operations, including offensives directed at the main American and South Vietnamese bases and strongholds. In II Corps area, the level was generally held down to the second stage of mobile guerrilla operations. In III Corps area, the area which includes Saigon, Viet Cong operations varied between the second and third stages, depending on whether these operations were being supported from the main bases or whether they were far away and mounted from slender resources. The war in IV Corps area was kept for the most part at the second stage, although since there were no North Vietnamese units stationed in the region, the Mekong Delta, there were places where the war had to proceed at the first level of strategic defensive coupled with political offensive.

During 1965 and 1966, the Allied forces paid a great deal of attention to War Zone D, north-east of Saigon, and in the following year War Zone C, north of Saigon in Tay Ninh province, and Phuoc Tuy province were cleared of main force Viet Cong regiments. Two American operations which had a telling effect on the Viet Cong were *Cedar Falls* and *Junction City*. The former was aimed at eliminating the Viet Cong headquarters for the Saigon-Gia Dinh area which was located in the Iron Triangle, a patch of dense jungle and secondary growth some twenty miles north of Saigon. It took place in January-February 1967 and cost the Viet Cong over 2,000 men captured or killed and several hundred tons of supplies, much of which had been slowly transported down from North Vietnam. *Junction City* penetrated War Zone C with a strength of three U.S. divisions and was successful to the extent that it forced the Viet Cong High Command in the South, the Central Office for South Vietnam (COSVN), to withdraw for a short time into Cambodia along with a division or more of regular troops.

It seems probable that it was the success of these two operations in III Corps area which caused Giap to raise the stakes of the war by opening a new and bloody series of desperate attacks in I Corps area which forced General Westmoreland to transfer to the northern provinces a great part of those divisions and regiments which had comprised his mobile striking force in the southern region. The sharp increase in the infiltration rate of North Vietnamese units into South Vietnam which followed necessitated the establishment of several strong points such as Con Thien and Khe Sanh around which so much fighting took place later in 1967 and in early 1968. The Northern preponderance of troops in this region produced a similar effect to that achieved by Giap in the early stages of the Dien Bien Phu battle in that the American garrisons were penned in by numbers so great that the bases became unable to support patrol activity over a wide area and became preoccupied with defending themselves against siege. However Westmoreland's strategy was much sounder than Navarre's, and the availability of American air power over Khe Sanh ensured sufficient supplies and fire support to enable the defenders to hold out. Several rumours circulated to the effect that Giap himself was near Khe Sanh directing the tactical battle. On the face of things it seems most unlikely that a commander in chief would absent himself from the only headquarters from which he could control the whole of his army's activities in order to direct a relatively small part of the war in person. Apart from the lack of confidence in subordinates which such a move would imply, there are also severe problems of reputation and status at stake. First, Westmoreland was quite happy to leave the conduct of the battle to the local Marine commanders and second, in the event of a North Vietnamese defeat at Khe Sanh, Giap's reputation would have quickly sunk back to human proportions in many quarters where it was necessary for their survival to credit Giap with Papal infallibility in the field of military doctrine. As events turned out, Khe Sanh was not a North Vietnamese victory and the attempt to make it one cost Giap's troops heavy losses. Nothing more was heard of Giap's presence on the battlefield. Perhaps, had the result been a North Vietnamese triumph, we might have heard differently concerning Giap's whereabouts.

In the meantime, the level of revolutionary warfare in the Central Highlands, in II Corps area, had been escalated to the third stage by Giap, who opened attacks around the highlands airhead and base of Dak To. This swing of emphasis to a point some two hundred miles away from the northern battles showed that he had not forgotten how to use surprise and variety to keep the initiative in his own hands. Despite the relatively non-productive results for the North Vietnamese of these battles in the northern and central provinces, they served to set the stage for Giap's greatest success of the war— the *Tet* offensive.

By January 1968, American and South Vietnamese troops were at full stretch in forward deployment to meet both the offensives that Giap had already mounted and those which he might be expected to mount. To take up this forward position, troops had to be pulled away from the more mundane business of town patrolling, village searches and close security patrolling around the more populated areas. These towns and villages had not been the subject of major offensives before and so they ranked low on the American priority list. However, their importance in the strategy of the war as far as the Viet Cong are concerned has already been stressed. Some observers have claimed that the whole series of North Vietnamese offensives was launched purely to entice the Americans into forward positions so that the main blow could be delivered to the populated areas where the greatest numbers of persons, both within South Vietnam and without, would be impressed with the stamina and growing strength of the Communist forces. This rationale seems to involve too long a time frame and too many unpredictables for Giap to have considered it to be the main justification for his series of blows to the northern and central provinces. What seems more likely is that Giap, a good opportunist like all good strategists, saw a way of exploiting a series of tactical defeats and turning them into a strategic victory.

The wave of attacks which poured over all the main cities and towns of South Vietnam in February, during the celebrations of *Tet*, or the Lunar New Year, turned out to be very costly to Giap's own troops, as he must surely have expected. Captured documents have indicated strong evidence that the North Vietnamese had gone back to the doctrine of a general uprising which they had hoped to trigger off by these direct assaults on the seats of the South Vietnamese government. However, no such uprising took place and the population, or at least the majority who were not participating in the attacks, remained loyal to the government. In particular, the South Vietnamese Army did not begin to disintegrate as had the Vietnamese units which fought alongside the French in 1953 and 1954. Either the North Vietnamese leadership had been acting on the basis of over-optimistic assessments of their support amongst the Southerners, or general uprising had been some sort of propaganda used to spur on those who had to make the necessary sacrifice.

It is difficult to attempt to assess which of these factors was dominant. Possibly both were operating, but certainly the Hanoi leaders do face a continual problem of having to act on exaggerated information. Time after time reports of actions which are sent back to Hanoi are intercepted and prove to be totally unrelated to whatever reverses the Communist forces may have suffered. It seems a fair assumption that the High Command is aware of this problem and does not believe everything which is reported by its subordinate commanders, but this does not help Giap to decide whether he should divide a figure by two or by ten to get close to the truth.

However, these considerations may not be too relevant to the question of determining Giap's aim in the *Tet* offensive. By late 1967, the North Vietnamese Army was engaged in heavy fighting with the U.S. Army and was not faring very well. In order to get out of this predicament it seems only logical that Giap should direct his strategy towards his enemy's weakest point—American public opinion—in the hope of compelling some fundamental change in the American direction of the war. It merely remained then for Giap to choose a goal which was both within his resources and likely to impress not the military analysts but the average citizen who knows nothing more about the war than what he sees on his television screen. Consequently what he needed was something spectacular enough to dominate television attention long enough to make an impact of strength on the American public, but not so protracted as to show up his weaknesses. By overrunning the towns, Giap captured world public attention and shattered what confidence many people had left in American power to win a military victory in Vietnam. Of course, Giap was also running the risk that American reaction to his success might provoke additional American involvement in the war, but this danger was perhaps sufficiently unlikely to be ignored.

In the aftermath of the *Tet* offensive, President Johnson declared his retirement from office at the end of his current term and General Westmoreland was replaced by General Abrams. It is unlikely that Giap thought that he could, in effect, eject Johnson from office. Nonetheless, had the *Tet* offensive not taken place, it is quite probable that Johnson would still have run for office in the Presidental elections and that Westmoreland would be in command in Saigon. The

effect of this change of leadership within the United States has
been to make the concept of an American military victory in
Vietnam even more difficult to visualize, and to strengthen
within America the forces of accommodation and compromise.

American pursuit of peace talks is another sympton of
Washington's uneasiness over the war and its prospects after
the *Tet* offensive. Predictably the North Vietnamese have
made no concession in their demands for American withdrawal from South Vietnam, so that in late 1968 we had a
group of senior North Vietnamese telling a group of senior
Americans in Paris nothing more than what Hanoi had already
made public. Unless some most unexpected event occurs to
weaken the stance of the North Vietnamese, it is difficult to
see how peace talks can succeed without the Americans giving
way substantially on their present minimum demands.

Thus, at the present time, Giap has achieved a position of
great strength for the Communist cause. The capacity of
American forces in Vietnam has been shown to be very limited
in terms of completely neutralizing the forces of both the Viet
Cong and of the North Vietnamese, so that we may expect a
continuation of the present situation until either Hanoi or
Washington makes a fundamental change in policy. There
seems to be little incentive for Hanoi to make such a change,
and with the elimination of the peace candidates from the
American Presidental race, there appears to be no immediate
prospect of an American revision of war aims.

In this situation of relative deadlock, many new circumstances may arise to change the balance one way or the other.
Apart from courting American public opinion, Giap has to
worry about the effectiveness of the system of control inside
North Vietnam. This system may be a very tight one, but it is
already bearing a considerable strain. One day when he calls
for that extra ounce of sacrifice, it may not be forthcoming.
Giap must also adjust his strategy to his sources of supply and
contrive to balance out the effects of the Sino-Soviet dispute
on the materials available for his armies to fight with. Another

political collapse in South Vietnam could also have irretrievable consequences, but the ability of the Southerners to reorganize their state on more democratic lines while in the midst of a war suggests that, despite the disunity and shortcomings of Saigon politicians, the Southern war effort can continue for at least as long as the American.

However, for North Vietnam to have achieved this position of apparent deadlock after the total reverse of the Geneva settlement in 1954 represents a formidable feat of strategy. Throughout the course of the present struggle, Giap's decisions have been shown to be fundamentally correct and of greater wisdom than those of his rival, Truong Chinh. Perhaps these successes have helped to enhance Giap's political position and to prepare the way for his eventual succession to the position of Ho Chi Minh, his boyhood hero. He would face strong competition from Pham Van Dong and Le Duan at least, and these forces may very well incline him, like many another wise military leader, to accept the palms of victory and then graciously retire from the competition for power. It seems most unlikely that there will not be at least a small palm for Giap, no matter what eventuates in the next few years. Provided that he does nothing uncharacteristically foolish during this intervening time, he will have earned by his life's activities an honoured place amongst the founder-heroes of his own state and amongst the outstanding military commanders of history.

Conclusion

After a first look at Giap's life and character, one is tempted to draw attention to the impact of environment to explain his rise to fame and power. He was born at a time when a demand for nationalist leaders was beginning to grow and he came from a family which was sufficiently well off to see that his schooling was not stopped before his development had reached its peak, but not so wealthy that he inherited a conservative approach to politics. While he was still being educated, the ideas of nationalism were placed before him in a particularly convincing and inspiring way by old Phan Boi Chau, and the vehicle of the Communist Party offered him ample scope to work for what he believed to be important. The chaos of World War II helped the Communists to political predominance amongst the Vietnamese nationalist parties, and so Giap was placed in a position of direct confrontation with the returning colonial masters. The inconsistencies between French colonial aims and the degree of sacrifice which the French people were prepared to tolerate after 1945 seemed to assure Giap of victory, if only he could endure a few years of pressure until French energies were spent. The development of the Cold War has provided him with the support of two of the greatest powers, while the efforts of a third to unseat him have brought him close to the centre of the international stage in a key role.

Had any one of these events not happened in just this manner, then Giap would probably be relatively unknown to the world. Yet it is equally true to say that had Giap lacked the necessary ability to move with the powerful and treacherous tides of politics, war, and international relations, he would not have withstood the stresses which his rise to eminence has forced him to bear.

The Vietnamese education system in the 1930s was of high quality and intensely competitive. Giap's progress to the University of Hanoi and his record at the University have established his intellectual reputation as of an order comparable to those of the leaders of nations much more powerful than Vietnam. Possibly some of his professors would regard as a pity the unquestioning devotion he has shown in speeches and writings towards the principles of Communism. Had he embraced a less dogmatic political creed, the fruits of his mind may have been more abundant. However, Giap may have a mind which functions at its best when working within the confines of discipline. It is difficult to imagine how otherwise he could have endured the personal limitations of his career.

Allied with his intellect, Giap possessed the practical skill to put his thoughts into writing with clarity, simplicity and brevity. He did not have to wait until he was discovered by some other writer before his mental activities had become part of Vietnamese politics. Since 1940 he has rarely had to rely on his ability as an author to achieve his aims, but he has shown in recent publications that he has not lost the perception and incision required for good political journalism, albeit of a very didactic type.

His practical abilities go much further than writing, as has been shown by his military and political careers. Both roles have called for organizing abilities, judgment, capacity to delegate work to the people best fitted to handle it, tireless energy, and the ability to make those beneath him work a little harder for him than they would have for most other leaders.

The limitations of his talents, which have been revealed in

the course of his active life, are those one associates more with lack of professional or vocational training than of mental development. Had he not been thrown headlong into intense and important activities as soon as he had completed his first degree, he might have developed into a better commander and political leader. The tools of experience which Ho Chi Minh has been able to call on to overcome crises were gained during his thirty years of wandering, free from the encumbrances of heavy administrative responsibilities. Giap has not had this time for experimentation and learning from others, and his life has probably suffered as a result.

His military campaigns have shown his competence and his ability to learn from mistakes, both his own and those of others, rather than his strategic brilliance. His methods are usually carefully thought out before action commences, and his planning has been thorough. Catastrophes and administrative chaos are not characteristic of Giap's army in the way that high casualties are. Since 1951 he has made few errors, but in his twenty years of activity as a field commander there seems to be little display of the outstanding qualities which have made men such as Marlborough, Napoleon, Guderian or Mao of importance to the student of military affairs. It may be that, like many potentially great soldiers, Giap has not had his chance but, in view of the intensity of the wars he has been fighting since 1946, this seems difficult to believe. He must be remembered for two great decisions: first, his move into the more remote parts of Tonkin in 1952-53 and second, his decision to fight a major battle at Dien Bien Phu. In each of these cases he has shown unquestionable mastery of the strategic situation. However, we read his books in vain for any contribution to strategic principles and the record of his mis-judgments is as well stocked as those of many commanders who have now been forgotten by the world.

Similar traits are noticeable in his political career. Giap has held positions of supreme responsibility at difficult times such as in 1946 and 1955-7, and he has discharged their duties rigorously and efficiently. Yet in thirty years within the leading echelon of the Vietnamese Communist Party, he has produced little to set him apart from other *apparatchiks*. His slightly bourgeois image has a touch of individuality about it, but it is difficult to see him developing the political skills to give him the support which more charismatic Vietnamese figures have enjoyed. Again, these remarks may be offset because Giap of necessity has been under the shadow of Ho for most of his life, and we could see a new image if Ho were to pass off the scene. However, patterns of conformity established over a generation of service to one leader are not easily broken, and we may well see little further development of Giap's political stature.

Where Giap's life has been of outstanding importance is in his ability to combine the roles of senior politician and top soldier. He has exploited his gifts in these two fields with great dexterity and has made himself of vital importance to Ho Chi Minh. Giap would be a very difficult man for the *Lao Dong* to replace, for who else in North Vietnam could be relied upon to lead the Army with a combination of such skill and loyalty to the wishes of the Party executive? In times of political crisis, what alternative Minister for the Interior could control popular unrest with firm political purpose, backed by the *ultima ratio* of force? Of all the lessons which are to be learned from studying the life of this man, perhaps the most significant are shown in his fusion of these two fields which, in Western societies, are normally kept apart. The separation of political power and military force is an essential feature of a liberal system of government, but when such a government sends its soldiers against a man like Giap, it finds that they commence their task with a handicap which few survive for long.

A Note on Sources

The quantity of literature on Vietnam now available has far exceeded that amount which can be studied by any one scholar and, unless one has the benefit of many years' experience of Vietnam, one is forced to be highly selective in reading about the affairs of this country. Joseph Buttinger claims that there are several thousand books on Vietnam now in existence and so the skeletal nature of the list given below must be emphasized. Writings on Vietnam vary greatly in their scope and quality, and a certain amount of caution is a necessary accompaniment to research in this field. The items listed below are generally the most reliable accounts which have stood up to detailed examination and criticism and most have been proved to be sound in fact and interpretation. Many of the publications from Hanoi are little more than propaganda in some parts, but the facts related in other parts show few signs of disparity with non-Communist sources and a remarkable degree of agreement with other Communist writings of different authorship. Hence, if one is interested in the early life of Ho Chi Minh and the rise of the Indo China Communist Party, *Days with Ho Chi Minh*, Foreign Languages Publishing House, Hanoi, 1962, cannot be ignored without leaving wide gaps in one's knowledge of the pre-1945 years. This list concentrates on material relating to Giap, his writings, political environment, battles and strategy.

Ainley, Henry. *In Order to Die*. Burke, London, 1955. A first hand account of the war in the early 1950s, concentrating on Cochin China and Cambodia.

Armbruster, Frank E., Raymond D. Gastil, Herman Kahn, William Pfaff, Edmund Stillman. *Can We Win In Vietnam?* Pall Mall, London; Frederick A. Praeger, New York, 1968. A most informative debate on the strategic issues of the Vietnam war, including treatment of the policies of North Vietnam as well as those of the U.S.A., prospects for the success of the present policies and suggestions for improvements. Unfortunately, over-optimistic conclusions are drawn from faulty data.

Bodard, Lucien. *The Quicksand War: Prelude to Vietnam*. Faber and Faber, London; Little, Brown, Boston, 1967. A translation of a French journalist's somewhat sensational account of events in Vietnam in the late 1940s and early 1950s—particularly good for the border battles of 1950 and for Saigon politics of the period.

Breaking Our Chains: Documents on the Vietnamese Revolution of August, 1945. Foreign Languages Publishing House, Hanoi, 1960. Contains significant documents issued by the Viet Minh relating to their accession to power in 1945.

Buttinger, Joseph. *Vietnam: A Dragon Embattled*. 2 Vols. Frederick A. Praeger, New York, 1967. The most comprehensive work on the politics of Vietnam since the late nineteenth century. Buttinger has a tendency to give uneven treatment to the major issues, but in the absence of other comparable works, this book is to be commended for its compass and scholarship.

Cole, Allan B. (ed.). *Conflict in Indo China and International Repercussions: A Documentary History, 1945-1955*. Cornell University Press, Ithaca, N.Y., 1956. Gives the fullest presentation of the documents relating to the war and summarizes the main phases with skill.

Democratic Republic of Vietnam. *The Democratic Republic of Vietnam*. Foreign Languages Publishing House, Hanoi,

1960. An official handbook on North Vietnam containing a brief official history of the Vietnamese people and a description of the major facets of life in North Vietnam today, including official attitudes to the war in the South.

Democratic Republic of Vietnam. *Vietnam's Fight Against Fascism, 1940-1945*. Paris, 1948. The Viet Minh account of internal politics during the Japanese occupation.

Devillers, Philippe. *Histoire du Viet-Nam de 1940 à 1952*. Editions du Seuil, Paris, 1952. An excellent account of the events of 1945-1950 by an author who knows Vietnam well through his own experience.

Devillers, Philippe and Jean Lacouture. *La fin d'une guerre: Indochine 1954*. Editions du Seuil, Paris, 1960. *End of a War: Geneva, 1954*. Frederick A. Praeger, New York, 1969. A full political and military history of the French campaign against the Viet Minh with excellent treatment of the Geneva conference.

Fall, Bernard B. *Street Without Joy: Insurgency in Indochina* (rev. ed.). Stackpole, Harrisburg, 1966. An indispensable interpretation of the French campaign in Indo China.

 The Two Viet-Nams: A Political and Military Analysis (2nd rev. ed.). Frederick A. Praeger, New York, 1967. A political and military analysis of the two Vietnamese states describing their political organization, economic problems and the effects of the war on each.

 The Viet-Minh Regime. Cornell University Press, Ithaca, N.Y., 1956. A very detailed study of North Vietnamese politics and organization.

 Hell in a Very Small Place. J. B. Lippincott, Philadelphia, 1966. The most detailed account of the battle of Dien Bien Phu—possibly the best piece of scholarship produced by Fall.

Gittinger, J. Price. 'Communist Land Policy in North Vietnam', in *Far Eastern Survey*, XXVII, August 1959, pp. 113-26. An excellent report on land reforms in North Vietnam.

Gosselin, Charles. *L'empire d'Annam*. Perrin, Paris, 1904. An

interesting account of the early years of the French col-
onialization of Indo China by a French officer who took
part.
Hall, D. G. E. *A History of South East Asia* (2nd ed., 3rd ed.,
1968). Macmillan, London, 1964; St. Martins, New York,
1964. An outstanding general history of the area with
some most useful chapters on Vietnam.
Hammer, Ellen J. *The Struggle For Indochina, 1940-1955*.
Stanford University Press, Stanford, Calif., 1956. A
thorough study of the years 1945-53. One of the best detailed accounts of French and Vietnamese politics during
the war against the Viet Minh.
Hoang Quang Binh. 'In Yunnan', in *Days with Ho Chi Minh*.
Foreign Languages Publishing House, Hanoi, 1962, pp.
148-162. An important account of Ho's activities in Yunnan after his return from Moscow, 1938-40.
Hoang Van Chi. *From Colonialism to Communism: A Case
History of North Vietnam*. Frederick A. Praeger, New
York, 1964. An account of Vietnamese affairs, particularly
during the 1950s by an anti-Communist who spent some
years under Viet Minh rule in the North. Generally reliable
but with occasional slips.
Honey, P. J. *Communism in North Vietnam: Its Role in the
Sino-Soviet Dispute*. M.I.T. Press, Cambridge, Mass.,
1963. This detailed analysis of North Vietnam's difficulties
in following 'the middle path' is preceded by a valuable
general analysis of North Vietnamese politics and political
leaders.
      (ed.) *North Vietnam Today: Profile of a Communist
Satellite*. Frederick A. Praeger, New York, 1962. Articles
previously published in the *China Quarterly* by leading
writers on Vietnam, treating, *inter alia*, the relations
between the Communist leaders. The following articles are
particularly useful: Philippe Devillers. 'The Struggle for the
Unification of Vietnam'.
      P. J. Honey. 'The Position of the DRV
Leadership and the Succession to Ho Chi Minh'.

Bernard B. Fall. 'Power and Pressure Groups in North Vietnam'.

'Revolt of the Intellectuals in North Vietnam'. *The World Today*, Vol. XIII, No. 6, June 1957.

'North Vietnam's Party Congress'. *The China Quarterly*, No. 4, Oct.-Dec. 1960.

Lancaster, Donald. *The Emancipation of French Indochina*. Oxford University Press, London, 1961. An excellently written study of the major events in Indo China between 1945 and 1954 by a British diplomat who was stationed in Saigon in the early 1950s.

Laniel, Joseph. *Le drame indochinois: De Dien Bien Phu au pari de Genève*. Plon, Paris, 1957. Laniel was provoked into writing this book by General Navarre's own account and sets forth his defence of his policy in 1953-54.

Navarre, Henri. *Agonie de l'Indochine*. Plon, Paris, 1956. The French commander's account of the confusion and catastrophe which enveloped the Expeditionary Corps during 1953-54.

Ngo Van Chieu. *Journal d'un combattant Viet-Minh*. Editions du Seuil, Paris, 1955. A good description of the experiences of a Viet Minh soldier.

Nguyen Khanh Toan. 'Meeting Ho Chi Minh in the Soviet Union', in *Days with Ho Chi Minh*. Foreign Languages Publishing House, Hanoi, 1962, pp. 139-47. A revealing account of Ho's activities in Moscow in the 1930s and of his return to the Far East in 1938.

O'Ballance, Edgar. *The Indo-China War 1945-1954: A Study in Guerilla Warfare*. Faber & Faber, London, 1964. This book contains little that is not in Fall's *Street Without Joy*, and makes some spectacular errors such as fighting the battle of Vinh Yen as if Vinh Yen were on the south side of the Red River instead of being to the north.

Roy, Jules. *The Battle Of Dien Bien Phu*. Faber & Faber, London; Harper & Row, New York, 1965. An account of the battle with detailed treatment of the events which caused it, based on personal interviews and experience. Indispensable for an understanding of the problems faced by Navarre in making his plan.

Salmon, Malcolm. *Focus on Indo-China*. Foreign Languages Publishing House, Hanoi, 1961. An historical account of politics in Vietnam, Laos and Cambodia written in Hanoi by a journalist of pronounced Communist sympathies. Nonetheless it is readable and presents another case which ought to be considered.

Tanham, George K. *Communist Revolutionary Warfare: From the Vietminh to the Viet Cong* (rev.ed.). Frederick A. Praeger, New York, 1967. An analysis of the tactics, organization, administration and political direction of the Viet Minh armed forces.

Thai Lan. *Ai Giet Trung Tuong Nguyen Binh (Who Killed Major General Nguyen Binh)*. Saigon, 1960. Purports to be a confidential account of internal feuds within the Viet Minh which led to the death of Nguyen Binh. Some of the more checkable details are correct and the narrative confirms other less detailed accounts of Nguyen Binh's death.

Tongas, Gerard. *J'ai vécu dans l'enfer communiste au Nord Viet-Nam et j'ai choisi la liberté*. Debresse, Paris, 1960. The author, a former Viet Minh sympathizer, relates his experiences under Viet Minh rule after 1954 and his change of cutlook to strong opposition towards the Vietnamese Communists.

Tournoux, J. R. *Secrets d'état*. Plon, Paris, 1960. An overdrawn account of the drama of French policy towards Indo China.

Trinquier, Roger. *Modern Warfare: A French View of Counterinsurgency*, Frederick A. Praeger, New York, 1964. The story of a former commander of French commandos who operated behind the Viet Minh lines, told with great frankness.

Truong Chinh. *Primer for Revolt: The Communist Takeover in Viet-Nam*. Frederick A. Praeger, New York, 1963. A reprint of the classic Viet Minh manual of political and military strategy.

Vo Nguyen Giap. *People's War People's Army*. Foreign Languages Publishing House, Hanoi, 1961; Frederick A. Praeger, New York, 1962. An over-rated miscellany of propaganda exercises which includes a useful appendix on Dien Bien Phu.

'Ho Chi Minh, Father of the Viet Nam Revolutionary Army', in *Days with Ho Chi Minh*. Foreign Languages Publishing House, Hanoi, 1962, pp. 181-230. This article which is nominally about Ho Chi Minh, tells far more about Giap's early years in the Communist movement than about Ho. It is well written and the details show close correspondence with other Viet Minh accounts of these years.

Nhat Lanh Dien So Va Thu Dong Vien. Nha Xhat Ban Su That, Hanoi, 1963. A collection of Giap's speeches, proclamations and writings.

Once Again We Will Win. Foreign Languages Publishing House, Hanoi, 1966. A collection of articles and speeches published for propaganda purposes.

Récit de la résistance vietnamienne, 1925-1945, par Vo Nguyen Giap (et al.). Edited by I. Puiseux, Francois Maspero, Paris, 1966. A collection of writings and speeches by Viet Minh leaders, including Giap.

Big Victory Great Task. Frederick A. Praeger, New York, 1968. A reprint of Giap's articles in *Nhan Dan* exhorting the people of North Vietnam to yet greater efforts in the war against the South.

Vu Anh. 'From Kunming to Pac Bo', in *Days with Ho Chi Minh*. Foreign Languages Publishing House, Hanoi, 1962, pp. 163-80. An interesting account of Ho's movements in southern China and of the selection of the Pac Bo cave as the first headquarters on Vietnamese soil.

Chronology of major events
in the life of Giap

1912 Birth of Vo Nguyen Giap, An Xa, Quang Binh Province.
1924 Giap enters *Lycée National*, Hue. *Tan Viet* Party founded.
1926 Giap meets Phan Boi Chau, reads Ho Chi Min's *Colonialism on Trial*, expelled from *Lycée National*.
1927 Giap joins Communist wing of *Tan Viet*.
1930 Yen Bay and associated uprisings. Giap imprisoned. Left wing of *Tan Viet* joins Indo China Communist Party.
1937 Giap completes his *licence en droit* at Hanoi University and becomes a Communist journalist.
1938 Giap begins post-graduate studies at Hanoi.
1938(?)Giap's first marriage.
1940 Giap and Pham Van Dong escape to China and join Ho Chi Minh. Japanese occupation of Vietnam. Giap forms his first guerrilla platoon (October) and from hence forward commands the Communist Armed Forces.
1941 Giap returns to Vietnam (Pac Bo) and attends the foundation of the *Viet Minh*. Later moves to Lam Son with some hundred soldiers.
1942 Formation of the *Dong Minh Hoi* (October).
1943 Giap's armed propaganda teams number several hundred. His first wife dies.
1944 Giap moves to Cho Don, forms first platoon of National Liberation of Vietnam and attacks French at Khai Phat and Na Ngan (December).

1945   Japanese imprison French administration (March).
        Viet Minh move from Lam Son to Tan Trao, and
        seize power in North Vietnam (August). Giap becomes
        Minister for the Interior.

1946   Giap dropped from Ho's cabinet, but in effect controls
        Hanoi regime (May-October). Giap re-marries and
        becomes Minister for National Defence.
        Outbreak of hostilities (November), leading to Giap's
        flight into the Viet Bac region (December).

1947   Giap narrowly evades capture during Valluy's Viet
        Bac offensive (October).

1948   Giap compels Valluy to withdraw the Bac Kan garri-
        son (August).

1949   Giap remains on defensive and harasses Lao Kay and
        Route 4. Ho introduces nation-wide conscription.

1950   Chinese Communists close up to Vietnamese border
        and supply substantial aid to Giap who forms four
        infantry divisions. Attacks on Lao Kay (April), Dong
        Khe changes hands twice (May), complete rout of
        French in border region (September-October).

1951   Giap's Red River delta offensive. Battles of Vinh Yen
        (January), Mao Khe (March), Day River (May-June).
        Nguyen Binh, *Viet Minh* leader in the South assassin-
        ated (October). De Lattre occupies Hoa Binh (Novem-
        ber).

1952   Giap forces French to quit Hoa Binh (February),
        launches offensive into North-West Tonkin (October),
        but fails to capture Na San.

1953   Three *Viet Minh* divisions enter Laos and are blocked
        on the Plain of Jars (May). Giap orders withdrawal
        to Vietnam. Navarre forms his plan (June), success-
        fully evacuates Na San (August) and occupies Dien
        Bien Phu (November). Giap decides to respond and
        concentrates four divisions.

1954   Giap launches attack on Dien Bien Phu (March-May).
        Geneva conference (April-July). Giap returns to
        Hanoi (October). Land Reform begins in the North.

1956   Giap denounces the excesses of the Land Reform
        (October) and quells disturbances in Nghe An
        Province with troops.

1957   Giap withdraws troops from Nghe An, disappears from public view.

1958   Phu Loi incident.

1959   Giap leads North Vietnamese protests over the Phu Loi incident and publishes *Dien Bien Phu*. Guerrilla attacks in the South intensify.

1960   Vietnamese edition of *People's War, People's Army* published. National Liberation Front founded.

1961   Foreign language editions of *People's War, People's Army* published.
        Battalion-sized *Viet Cong* attacks in South Vietnam.

1962   Laos crisis.

1963   Fall of Diem.

1964   Gulf of Tonkin incident, U.S. bombing of North Vietnam commences. Regimental sized *Viet Cong* attacks in South Vietnam.

1965   Massive American commitment to South Vietnam. Giap sends North Vietnamese regulars to the South in formed divisions but the Americans thwart his attempt to divide the South into two.

1966   Mutual escalation and military stalemate in South Vietnam. *Once Again We Will Win* published.

1967   Khe Sanh besieged. Giap's articles in *Nhan Dan* and *Quan Doi Nhan Dan* published (English translation *Big Victory, Great Task*).

1968   *Tet* offensive. Paris peace talks organized.

1969   Paris peace talks commence to discuss the war.

Index

215